Customer Service
Eagles

by Joe Constance

Cover Design by Elizabeth Beckman
beckmanli@charter.net

Interior Layout by Stacey Willey

Contributing Editor
Ward Rantala, CEBS, ChFC, CTFA, AEP
Award Production
wrantala@charter.net

Published by
Constant Training
Marquette, Michigan

Print Coordination
Globe Printing, Inc., Ishpeming, Michigan
www.globeprinting.net

ISBN # 978-0-9800607-0-6

Second Printing May 2008
Third Printing August 2008
Fourth Printing November 2008

Key word listings:

1. Customer service 2. Customer relations 3. Employee training

This book is dedicated to:

My wife Ann, without whom it may have never been started, and certainly would never have been finished. She is the motivators' motivator who keeps me happy and healthy!

My parents Rose and Don, who taught me to stand up, literally and figuratively, and gave me the confidence to venture out into the world, take risks, make mistakes, and still survive.

My sons Adam and Alex. I am proud of both of you.

Acknowledgements:

I would like to sincerely thank the following individuals for bringing this book to life:

Sam Behm, who took many hours of audio tapes and ten years of notes and put it into a logical, readable format. Nicole Walton for her EAGLE efforts in proofing the copy (many times!). Doug Russell, Diana Constance, Beverly Jones, and Don St. Germaine for their reviews and suggestions. The customer service EAGLES I have met and talk about in this book. Finally to all my past employees, business partners, and customers. You provided my REAL education and I apologize for my MANY mistakes!

Table of Contents

"The bad news is, our customers hate us. The good news is, we have a lot fewer customers than we used to!"

> *Too much of a good thing… can be wonderful.*
>
> Mae West (1893 – 1980) Actress, sex symbol

Introduction

Go into any establishment—a restaurant, retail store, non-profit organization or government office and observe the service you receive. How many times would you rate that service "excellent?" Four out of five (I'm being generous here) organizations provide service that can be described as "mediocre" at best. In fact, when we do get service we consider extraordinary or excellent, it really stands out. Why? Because it is extremely RARE. As Hal Becker says in his book *Lip Service*, "Everyone talks about the importance of customer service, but nobody does anything about it."

Every single one of us is "in" some form of customer service. We are all in the people business. I challenge you to name one person who earns a paycheck for a living, who is not in the people-pleasing business. Restaurants? Obviously. But how about doctors? People have a lot more healthcare choices these days; if they are not happy, they will switch. Lawyers? Yes, competition in that field is fierce. Teachers? You bet. And garbage collectors, carpenters, landscapers, artists, custodians, truck drivers, and dentists. Even government workers, once notorious for complacent, if not rude service, are working to improve service to their customer - the taxpayers who pay their wages. Even if you are an employee who never deals face-to-face with an outside customer, you still have to provide good service to your employer and your fellow employees or you'll be out of a job.

Excellent customer service isn't rocket surgery folks (nei-

> *I hate quotations.*
>
> Ralph Waldo Emerson (1803 – 1882) American essayist, poet

ther rocket science nor brain surgery!). It's basic, common sense. But in our hustle and bustle high-stress world, we forget the basics. Too often, we forget until it's too late. Our business slowly erodes, we capture less and less market share, our margins dwindle to non-profit status, and we wonder what happened. It's easy to point the finger and blame Wal-Mart, gas prices, the economy, the current administration, the internet, or poor employees. It's much harder to look in the mirror and ask, "Have we done this to ourselves?" or "How much better could we have served our customers?"

So why should you care? Why do you want to provide the best possible customer service? The benefits to you:

- It is one of the best forms of job security you can have.
- Personal pride in knowing you have done your best.
- If you rely on "tips" in your job, there is a direct connection to the amount of cash you take home every day.
- Terrific service skills require having important people skills, which transfer to almost every area of your life.
- Great service ultimately gets rewarded with better pay and more rewarding jobs.
- When you provide higher levels of service, stress is lower and job satisfaction increases.
- It is much more fun to interact with customers who are happy.

I have focused on making this book "user friendly" by keeping it simple and practical. It includes hundreds of time-tested tools and ideas to improve your service. If you get just one great idea, wouldn't it be worth it? How much is one idea worth? Ask Bill Gates! It is my hope and expec-

> *Customer service skills provide a master key to success in all areas of your life.*
>
> Paul Timm – Independent consultant, trainer

tation you will get many useful ideas to implement right now—strategies that will make your work and life less stressful and more fruitful.

In the seminars I give on achieving customer service excellence, participants continuously ask for a book on the ideas we cover. I get e-mails regularly asking for books and/or tapes. So, in large part, one of the reasons I wrote this book was to provide them—and you—good service by filling that need. If you were a men's clothing retailer and your customers kept asking for polka-dot pants, you'd stock polka-dot pants, wouldn't you?

Above all, have fun. As I said before: this isn't rocket surgery, so have a blast and get ready to soar to new heights!

NOTE:

This book is designed for easy use as a training program or course for any organization. It is divided into thirteen chapters which can be read in less than thirty minutes each. I have shamelessly swiped a terrific idea from Benjamin Franklin, who used a system of thirteen virtues. He practiced one each week for thirteen weeks, then repeated them four times a year. Each chapter can be "assigned reading" for the week, with one of the four activities at the end used as a way to incorporate the ideas into the organization. Since there is no finish line in the pursuit of customer service excellence, the chapters can and should be repeated regularly and indefinitely.

So let's begin, and **may the course be with you!**

> *In God we trust – all others bring data.*
>
> Dr. W. Edwards Deming (1900 – 1993) American statistician

"My most valuable business skill? I know how to make you feel like the most important person in the whole world!"

The magic begins with you.

Walt Disney (1901-1966) Founder of the Walt Disney Company

1

Eagles versus Ducks

Two types of individuals stand out in the world of customer service: Eagles and ducks. Let's define the terms we are using and why.

EAGLES

Almost everyone has a positive opinion of Eagles. They symbolize power, strength, intelligence, and single-mindedness of purpose. The Eagle is synonymous with America and all the values we hold dear.

We use the term "Eagle eye" to describe someone with keen vision and the skill to fixate on a target and hold it, unwavering, until the goal is achieved. An Eagle in golf is that rare occurrence: two strokes better than par. If you have ever made an Eagle in golf, the thrill is memorable (or so they tell me!). In the Boy Scouts, the rank of Eagle Scout is reserved for those rarest-of-rare individuals who exhibit the highest degree of character and integrity through performance. A list of Eagle Scouts includes leaders in every segment of society and is a veritable "Who's Who" in America: Willie Banks, Olympian and former world record holder in the triple and long jump; William C. DeVries, M.D., surgeon who transplanted the first artificial heart; Gerald Ford, 38th

> *Everyone brightens up a room – some when they enter and some when they leave.*
>
> Mark Twain (1835 – 1910) Humorist, writer

President of the United States; Neil Armstrong, first person to set foot on the moon; J. Willard Marriott, Jr., Chairman of the Board and President of Marriott Corporation; Steven Spielberg, director & producer; Sam Walton, Founder of Wal-Mart.

An Eagle is one who rises to the occasion, one who can always be counted on. Eagles take initiative and personal responsibility. It is an Eagle who says, "Put me in, coach!" Eager and confident, an Eagle looks for opportunity. When it comes to customer service, an Eagle is "Johnny on the spot."

DUCKS

And when we think of ducks (besides food for Eagles)? Ducks spend most of their time paddling 'round the pond, heads down, butts in the air, looking for fish. Ducks are timid and fearful. Ducks get nervous and panic easily. Customer service ducks are noticeable by their very absence. Like when you're in a department store, searching in vain for help and the only clerk in the area has her head down, stocking shelves, ignoring you, "ducking" her responsibility.

I first came upon the Eagle/duck concept in college working at a bank. I worked at the main office and was one of three on the teller line. There was a revolving door customers came through to get into the lobby, so you'd see the door start to go around before you saw a customer come in. I was on one end, "Lou" on the other, and "Donna" in the middle. When that door started to revolve, Donna would often turn around and work on her night deposits or mail, or go get supplies or a drink from the water cooler. There were times when we actually caught her ducking down in her teller

> *84.6% of all statistics have no basis in actual facts.*
>
> Joe Constance (1955 -) Entrepreneur

cage. We called her "the duck" because she was regularly "ducking" out of taking care of customers.

Most organizations have some ducks—people who spend more time getting out of work than getting work done. Ducks aren't bad people, mind you; it just may be they are in positions ill-suited to their personalities. They may need training or a different job.

When it comes to taking care of customers, it is a duck who says "It's not my job..." "I don't know..." "That's not our policy..." "No, we don't have that..." and "Sorry, we're closing soon..." It is the Eagle who says, "Sure, I can help you!" "I can take care of that for you," and "I'd be happy to stay past closing. What can I do for you?"

Now that you're thinking about Eagle-versus-duck behavior and attitudes, I'll bet you can think of many instances when you've encountered both Eagles and ducks. Which would you prefer to do business with or deal with? Look at some of the Eagles and ducks in the following personal experiences:

John "Curly" Wagner has worked in and run the family tire business for more than forty years. I have done business with him since I bought my first car. One day I drove to his shop, went in and told Curly I needed four new tires. He came out, looked at my current tires, and told me point-blank, "Joe, these tires are good for another year. They don't need to be replaced yet." It is an EAGLE that talks customers *out* of making purchases, even if it isn't in their best short-term interest. It is an EAGLE that builds long-term relationships by earning the trust of their customers over time. I trust Curly without question!

> *Everyone is a good example of customer service.*
> *You are either a good example of good service,*
> *or you are a good example of bad service.*
>
> Joe Constance (1955 -) Entrepreneur

My wife called me one Saturday morning when I was on the road. She was frantic, saying, "The wind storm has blown the roof off of our house!" Trying to calm her down, I had her call Scott White, our insurance agent, at Hetrick & Associates. Being Saturday morning, the office was closed, so she called Scott's home. His wife said Scott was across town at a sporting event with the kids, but she would get to him right away. Scott was at our house thirty minutes later assuring my wife he would take care of everything. (Note: The roof *didn't* blow off—the shingles did!)

I was in an office supply store in Connecticut, and the person at the cash register had a nameplate stating her title as "Operations Supervisor." I told her I was in town for the day and asked if she knew of a health club nearby. With a blank expression she said, "I have no clue," and turned to ring up my purchases. That was it! No options or offer to help. But she *was* right about one thing: SHE HAD NO CLUE! Quack-Quack!

At the Winston-Salem Visitors Bureau in North Carolina I saw information regarding tours of the RJ Reynolds house. I asked the woman at the desk for directions. Her name was Elaine, and she told me the Reynolds house was closed on Mondays. I was disappointed since it was the only day I had free. Elaine said she would be happy to see if anyone was available to give me a tour. After two phone calls, she located someone who gave me a private tour. An EAGLE effort all the way!

I was in a large sporting goods store looking for racquetball equipment. A group of five employees stood chatting while I wandered around and around looking for racquetball stuff to no avail. No assistance was offered. I walked by the group on my way out, to a store that would actually help

> *Normal is nothing more than a cycle on a washing machine.*
>
> Whoopi Goldberg (1955 -) Comedian, actor

me. They lost $225 that moment, without even knowing it. (I returned to that town two years later and they were no longer in business! That duck pond had dried up!)

I walked into a grocery store at 6:00 a.m. looking for a banana for breakfast. Finding no bananas in the produce section, I asked the cashier if they had any. She said they received some deliveries that morning and she would go back and check. She came back with a whole bunch of bananas. They were green and hard as a rock, but she was still an EAGLE in my eyes!

I once observed Mitch Lazeren, an owner of a very successful Bonanza Steak House in my hometown, talking with one of his diners. The customer told Mitch he was having some electrical problem at his home. Mitch went to another table, brought over a man who was an electrician and introduced the two. Talk about flying like an Eagle!

Examples of Eagles and ducks are everywhere, and you see them every day if you look. The one thing setting Eagles apart from ducks is that Eagles look for ways to WOW customers. No matter what the customer wants, an Eagle finds a way to make it happen, or at least leaves the customer better than when he or she found him.

We must become more observant and more vigilant if we are to improve our customer service skills. The mental "anchors" of Eagles and ducks is a simple but effective way to help us with our observations. The next time you go into a department store, convenience store or government office, try to place their service people in either the Eagle or duck category. Do this not to *discriminate*, but to *differentiate*. This is not to say one person is good and the other bad. We are focusing on their *behavior* relative to delivering good

> *I can only please one customer per day.*
> *Today is not your day – tomorrow isn't*
> *looking good either.*
>
> Dilbert

customer service. In other words, observe their *actions and attitude*. Which actions are consistent with Eagle behavior? You will likely find most people are neither—they are in the "mediocre middle," neither ducks nor Eagles!

As we become more observant of Eagle and duck behavior outside our businesses, we naturally become more vigilant of Eagle and duck behavior within our organization. The training we do within our organization steers us toward producing more Eagles.

Perhaps Vince Lombardi explains best what it is to be an Eagle:

Excellence can be obtained if you...
Care more than others think is wise.
Risk more than others think is safe.
Dream more than others think is practical.
Expect more than others think is possible.

EAGLE EYE VIEW

- People have a positive impression of EAGLES.
- EAGLES stand for power, strength, and intelligence.
- EAGLES are un-common.
- EAGLES greet customers enthusiastically.
- EAGLES look for ways to help customers.
- EAGLES look for opportunity.
- EAGLES look for ways to WOW customers.
- Ducks ignore the customer.
- Ducks look for excuses or ways not to help.
- Ducks seek to avoid any extra effort.
- Ducks "duck for cover."

It's a jungle out there.

Tarzan

EXERCISE 1:1

Keep track of all the Eagles and ducks at each encounter you have as a customer for one full day. Most may be in the middle or "just ok," but Eagles and ducks stand out more. Keep track of what the Eagles did that you loved, and how the ducks fell short. Note how you feel about the organization based on that one experience.

EXERCISE 1:2

Answer this question: Why do I want to be an EAGLE? What are the benefits to me? What difference will it make in my work life and my personal life?

EXERCISE 1:3

What one idea in this chapter can I use that will have the most positive impact on service to my customers? What is my action plan, what will I do to make the needed change, and when?

EXERCISE 1:4

What one idea in this chapter can our organization implement to have the most positive impact on our customer service? What changes do we need to make? When and how will we go about implementing them?

When on earth, do as earthlings do.

Mork

Accept that some days you are the pigeon and some days you are the statue.

Dilbert

"The 8-track stereo is out of stock, the lime green leisure suit is out of stock, the Earth shoes, mood ring, and Disco Barbie are also out of stock. Would you like me to send you a new catalog, ma'am?"

> *It takes less effort to keep an old customer satisfied than to get a new customer interested.*
>
> Unknown

2

What do Customers Want?

My wife and I collect precious stones (okay, so they are only precious to us). We like to walk beaches and find stones that “look cool”. One day we went to a local rock shop to buy a rock polisher. We immediately found what we wanted. The owner of the shop came over and started to give us the history of rocks, Starting somewhere around five billion years ago! Neither of us was at all interested in this history, but that didn’t matter to this guy. He WANTED to tell us and proceeded to tell us, for at least ten minutes. We just looked at each other as he droned on. I tried to get him to sell us the polisher by asking if he had this specific model in stock. The owner quickly responded “yes”, and began again with the history—now only a few million years ago. As he went on and on I asked if he took credit cards. He again responded “yes,” and continued talking. We walked to the register as he followed, still talking. I gave him my credit card and he *still* talked while *slowly* processing our purchase. I don’t think he wanted us to leave! FINALLY he put our polisher in a bag and we ran out of the store. We will not go back into that store again unless we have a few extra hours.

A similar thing happened when trying to get help with my

> *You don’t get to be # 1 by treating the customer like # 2.*
>
> Unknown

computer problems. I called to talk to "professionals" and they instantly started speaking a language I didn't understand. Don't get me wrong, they WERE speaking English; I just couldn't understand all the technical jargon they threw at me. Not only did I not understand, but I had no *desire* to understand! All I wanted was for them to fix my problem. I don't need to know HOW it works or why; I just want it to work, period.

I finally found the right computer expert in Todd, who owns Career Academy. He treats me like the idiot I am (just kidding), by keeping things simple, fixing my problem, and sending me on my computing way. I am *happy*!

Great service—EAGLE service—then, is *personalized.* It's not a cookie-cutter answer, a set of procedures, or a solution in a box. It's giving the customer what they need - once we know what that is.

What do customers want? A study by Dr. Leonard Berry at Texas A&M University concluded there are five main factors in customer satisfaction. They are:

1. *Reliability*—the product or service is delivered as promised.
2. *Responsiveness*—an eagerness to help in a prompt manner.
3. *Assurance*—employee skill, knowledge, courtesy, and problem-solving skills.
4. *Empathy*—caring and relationship building.
5. *Tangibles*—the appearance of buildings, facilities, and informational materials.

> *Satisfaction" is the lowest level of acceptable service.*
>
> Jeffrey Gitomer – Business coach, author

I don't think anyone would argue with the list above. We all want those things—or do we? Not every customer wants to build a relationship, or even know anything about us. This study is probably the result of thousands of customer comments grouped together. But customers aren't groups—they're individuals.

What *do* customers want? I conduct a sixty-second survey in my seminars of the top-ten "turn-offs" and "turn-ons"—things customers either hate or love. I survey my seminar attendees because they're customer service experts. So are you. In fact, we are *all* customer service experts. Why? Because we are all customers! Do you know when someone gives you good service? Of course you do! You also know when you're dealing with someone who just doesn't care. Which feels better? It's critically important to recognize these feelings because, as we will discover, good feelings lead to long-term, positive relationships.

Now let's look at the things topping the list of what more than 10,000 customers consider bad service.

TOP TEN CUSTOMER SERVICE TURN-OFFS:

- Poor attitude—is rude or just doesn't care.
- Help or assistance is unavailable.
- Having to wait in long lines.
- Being put on "hold" for a long period of time.
- Slow or no response to complaints.
- Employees who ignore customers.
- Policies or rules that are inflexible or unfair.
- Poorly trained employees.
- Disorganization.
- Won't admit mistakes.

If we don't take care of our customers,
someone else will.

Unknown

There are several other things you could add, but these are the most consistent irritants. Now, was this rocket surgery? No. It's common sense, isn't it? And that's exactly what good customer service is: *common sense.* Unfortunately it's not necessarily *common practice.* What one person thinks is common sense, another would never consider. What irritates one customer may not irritate another. Some people go ballistic waiting in a line to pay, while other customers enjoy talking to other people in line and have no problem waiting.

Now let's look at the positive list. What did more than 10,000 customers say they liked?

TOP TEN CUSTOMER SERVICE TURN-ONS:

- Went out of their way to help.
- Did a little something extra.
- Were friendly and hospitable.
- Greeted me promptly.
- Called me by name.
- Cared about me.
- Appreciated me.
- Handled my problem.
- Anticipated my needs.
- Did what they said they would.

Again, no rocket surgery here, just a lot of good, common sense. Nor is it difficult.

Look at the "positive" list again. What do you observe? The one common denominator is simply one human being showing kindness and consideration to another. It is **human-to-human courtesy**. This is what builds relationships. Customers want to be greeted quickly. They want a warm, friendly, knowledgeable person available to talk to.

> *The hardest thing in the world to understand is the income tax.*
>
> Albert Einstein (1879 – 1955) Theoretical physicist

They want choices and they want a clean and safe environment.

What do customers want? The Gallup Organization, which has reportedly surveyed more than one billion customers, found the following:

1. Customers expect accuracy.
2. Customers expect availability.
3. Customers expect partnerships.
4. Customers expect advice.

All of the above make sense. Some results differ from other research and some are the same. We can relate to all of it though, by being customers ourselves.

So what does this all mean? What do customers really want? The difficult part is that *not everyone wants the same thing*. Every customer is unique in needs and wants. Eagles understand this and are always looking for ways to meet and exceed customer expectations. This basic but critical awareness is what separates Eagles from ducks!

I was in the restaurant business for many years. During that time I learned some customers want to be left alone in a quiet corner and have their server be invisible, while others come in and want to be entertained as they eat. Some may even want a server by their table during the whole dining experience. Because of this, I would tell my employees that you can't treat every customer the exact same way. If we made a list of ten things to do with every customer, some of those items would make for happy customers, but some would irritate others. The key is to treat customers the way *they* want to be treated.

Some customers want a lot of details; others don't want any. Some customers want you to spend all day with them;

> *Sometimes Eagles land in duck ponds.*
>
> Joe Constance (1955 -) Entrepreneur

others want to get in and out in under a minute. Some customers want to socialize and others don't. I could go on for a hundred pages citing research study after research study on what customers want, but I think you get the drift. EVERYBODY potentially wants something different! Terrific service involves determining customer wants and needs and then treating them accordingly.

BEWARE OF ASSUMPTIONS

What do customers want when they come into a restaurant? Food, duh! But wait—for years many customers would come into my restaurant and CHOOSE to wait, even though they wanted to eat right away! Maybe some customers want more than just food!?

Jill Boroughf is a customer service Eagle. Customers would regularly wait thirty minutes for an open table in her section rather than be seated elsewhere immediately. If we assume all they came in for was food, then that just doesn't make any sense. Obviously, these customers wanted more than just physical nourishment. Some wanted to be entertained; some wanted to connect with a friend. Jill was outstanding at making friends and building relationships. She was an outstanding server who used lots of humor with a personal touch. She also made a LOT of money in tips, significantly more than many other servers!

One other crucial point to consider is to assume a customer ACTUALLY KNOWS what they want! This can be a big mistake. Many times customers either have no clue what they want or need, or at best, have just a few ideas. They rely on us to help them make *informed* decisions. This

> *I can't say I was ever lost, but I was bewildered once for three days.*
>
> Daniel Boone (1724 – 1820) Pioneer, hunter

process is part relationship building and part trust building. It's also why I believe smaller specialty stores can and do compete very effectively with the "big box" stores. They can provide so much more when it comes to product knowledge and helpful advice. True to the saying - big isn't always better.

I go into my local sports shop looking for running shoes. The employee first wants to see my current shoes. I am initially a bit confused, but he explains he can tell my running style by looking at my soles. Immediately, he tells me I am a "pronator". After asking me a number of other questions, he recommends a certain shoe for me.

Now picture me going into a typical "big box" store and telling the shoe department clerk that I am a pronator. He tells me that he doesn't care, as long as I don't do it in the store! NO CLUE!

Don't assume just by looking at a customer that you "know" them or their type. Many a great potential customer has been lost by being prejudged or when assumptions are made by the way they dress, their age, or their ethnicity. Don't assume every senior citizen doesn't have a high speed internet connection and hates to do business online. And don't assume the young kid looking for a gift has little or no money to spend.

God is dead.

Friedrich Nietzsche (1844 – 1900)

Nietzsche is dead.

GOD

EAGLE EYE VIEW

- *Every* customer is different.
- EAGLES treat customers the way the customers want to be treated.
- EAGLES are aware of the most common irritants, as well as the things customers love.
- EAGLES don't assume they automatically know what every customer wants or needs.
- EAGLES don't assume the customer knows what they want or need!

EXERCISE 2:1

Keep track of at least three customer service encounters you have this week when you are the customer. Was the employee able to give you exactly what you wanted and treat you the way you wanted to be treated? Or did you get the "canned" service experience—the exact same one they throw at every customer. If they were good at giving you what you wanted, how did they know and what did they do to determine it? What can you learn from them?

EXERCISE 2:2

Keep track of the customers you encounter in your work for one full day. Try to "read" your customers. Note how assumptions may get you in trouble or cost you satisfied customers when you misread them. What specifically can you do to avoid making the wrong assumptions? What specifically can you do to find out what they really want from you?

> *Let's make a dent in the universe.*
>
> Steve Jobs (1955 -) Co-founder of Apple Computer

EXERCISE 2:3

Pick five good customers and ask what they want from you. Ask what is most important to them. Ask what they want that they are not getting from you or your organization. Finally, ask them how you can improve your customer service. Meet as an employee group to discuss your findings and determine what can be implemented or changed to improve overall customer service.

EXERCISE 2:4

Contact five former customers who don't do business with you any longer or haven't for at least one year. Ask them what made them stop using your products or services. Ask them if there is anything you can do to have them "try" you again. As an employee group, review the reasons customers chose to go somewhere else and decide if there is anything you can do to reduce the number of unhappy or lost customers.

Human beings only use 10% of their brains. Ten percent! Can you imagine how much we could accomplish if we used the other 60%!

Ellen DeGeneres (1958 -) Actress, comedian

My formula for success? Rise early, work late, strike oil.

J. Paul Getty (1892 – 1976) American industrialist

"Before you can sell something, the customer has to like you! Did you remember to lick his face?"

You never get a second chance to make a first impression.

Will Rogers (1879-1935) Comedian, cowboy

3

First and Last(ing) Impressions

For more than ten years, when you walked into Margaritaville (my former restaurant's bar), you were greeted instantly with an enthusiastic hello and a big, genuine smile. Dotty and Penny are two customer service Eagles who took care of our valued customers and made sure their first impressions were positive. They were outstanding at making strangers comfortable and regulars feel appreciated. They talked, they listened, and they had lots of fun doing it.

First impressions are HUGE. Customers or prospects often accept or dismiss you based on this factor alone. Someone once said that it's hard to overcome a negative first impression, so why start with one?

No matter what business or organization you're in, customers form opinions of you long before they drive into your parking lot or walk in your door. First impressions are formed by advertising, appearance, reputation, staff, product and facility. If you neglect certain details—like fresh paint and cleanliness—customers may assume you have a careless attitude or are lazy. If you are in food service, they might assume the food isn't fresh or sanitary. It can mean the difference between whether or not they patronize your business.

> *You had me at hello.*
>
> - Renee Zellweger to Tom Cruise in Jerry Maguire

The devil's in the details! Let's look at how customers make first impressions and what we can do to make sure they are positive.

ADVERTISING

It definitely makes an impression. That is what we pay for - impressions. So, once again, pay very close attention to what those impressions are. What message is being communicated? Ask, "What is it saying about us?" The advertising message is your story, so make sure it's what you truly want your customers to know about you. Then make sure it's the truth! If you advertise fast service, guess what customers are going to expect? Or, if you advertise the friendliest place in town and the first person they meet is Glenda Grumpy, guess what happens to their first impression? Guess what happens to your advertising dollars?

APPEARANCE

Have you been to Disney World? If not, go there for the fun of it, and, if you're a serious student of excellent customer service, go there to observe. Watch and learn. You will see immaculate grounds, tended daily. Grass and shrubs are clipped to precision and perfection. Litter? No way! Despite a park full of tens of thousands of visitors—many of whom are children—you do not see litter. How is this possible?! Any trash accidentally dropped is whisked away immediately by an almost invisible team member. I say "invisible" because it happens so swiftly, silently, and effortlessly that you have to watch to catch it. These team members are everywhere, blending into the scenery. I tested this on one trip to see how long it would take them to pick up trash I

> *Great customer service begins with you smiling as they walk in, and ends with them smiling as they walk out.*
>
> Joe Constance (1955 -) Entrepreneur

dropped. I "littered" ten times at different locations. The quickest trash pick up was twelve seconds, and the longest was just over seven minutes!

Every building, fence, statue, and feature at Disney World looks brand new. You feel like it's opening day and you—you are the very first visitor. I marvel at this. How does Disney create this feeling?

I remember the first time I went to Walt Disney World. Walking out of the park that evening, in a state of exhausted euphoria, something unusual caught my eye. Atop a building on Main Street, painters were applying a new coat on the Victorian spindles of a widow's walk two stories up. I stood, puzzled. From my vantage point it looked fine—new, in fact. Why would they paint it now? They could wait years! Who would notice if the paint was getting a little dull or starting to peel? Who looks up there anyway? The answer: they do. They notice. They want every little detail to be *perfect*, for us, their guests.

The horse statues on Main Street are painted *every night*. Can you imagine the expense? How many other businesses would be tempted to post "DO NOT TOUCH!" signs? Not Disney. They know their guests enjoy touching the horses, so they encourage it by keeping them freshly painted.

What do we do when we have important company coming for dinner? We clean everything spic 'n' span. We get out the "good china." We do it out of pride and to make sure our company feels special. That's what Disney does so well. They make each and every guest feel special. What do guests do in return? They have fun, and they open their wallets. Is it magic?

Now let's talk about *your* facility—your parking lot, building, office, furnishings and lighting. We must look critically

> *We try to give people a great experience – hot, fresh memories.*
>
> Stan Parker – Krispy Kreme Donuts

at all of these areas, because they each send a message to your customers. Am I being picky? You bet! Just as your customers are, so must you be.

What your facility looks like makes an impression on your customers. What does it say about you? Is it neat and organized? Then they will likely assume you are too. Is the parking convenient and the entry way easy to access? They will assume you are accessible and easy to do business with as well. Are the colors and lighting friendly and welcoming? They will think you are too. They will come in, open to what you have to offer.

Put yourself in the following scenario: You're new in town. You need homeowner's insurance. Armed with the Yellow Pages, you drive to "Insurance-R-Us." The signage is poor. The parking lot entrance is difficult to find and navigate. Cars are parked haphazardly. Litter blows across the lot. There are weeds around the building. A sign on the door says, "Use other door." The office smells musty, the paint is dingy and the lighting is poor. The carpet hasn't been vacuumed in weeks, and the "high-traffic" area is obvious. The office area is a landslide of paperwork. Post-it notes paper the walls, their curled edges a sign they've been ignored for quite some time. The artificial plant in the corner needed dusting a year ago. The receptionist, who does not look up, has rap music playing loudly. What are you feeling? Do you have confidence in them? Is this a company you want to do business with? Can you see yourself coming back on a regular basis? Wouldn't they now have to go to extraordinary measures to earn your business?

Do all the good you can, by all the means you can, in all the ways you can, in all the places you can, as long as you ever can.

John Wesley (1703 – 1791) Anglican clergyman

Let me ask you this: how easy was it to visualize this office? Easy, huh? Sadly, we have all had similar experiences, and what happened?—it stuck in our minds, but for all the *wrong* reasons.

Now picture driving to the next insurance company listed in the Yellow Pages, Hetrick & Associates. There is easy access to the parking lot, which is neatly laid out with wide parking spaces. It is clean and well maintained. The shrubs are trimmed and healthy. Warm light glows through the front doors, which sparkle. The rugs in the vestibule and the carpet appear to be new. Well-cared-for green plants add warmth. There is a clean fragrance. Music plays softly. The entire office seems fresh. Sitting at a tidy, well-organized desk, the receptionist, who is wearing a name tag that identifies her as "Debbie," immediately looks up, smiles broadly, and says, "Hi! How are you? What can I help you with today?" How do you feel now? My guess is, you just found your new insurance agency.

Just as your mode of dress tells the world who you are, the way we "dress" our business creates a similar impression. Is this a friendly place? Does it instill confidence? Is it easy to do business here? Does it appear solid? Honest? Do the employees care? These are all questions the customer's subconscious asks. How you measure up determines whether or not they even walk in the door.

SOUNDS

What do customers first hear when they approach your building or department? Are they positive, uplifting sounds, or are they sounds that irritate or might disturb potential customers? Do customers hear employees complaining or managers yelling at people? Do they hear loud music that,

> *Mickey is picky.*
>
> Walt Disney (1901 – 1966) Founder of the Walt Disney Company

while the employees may love it, may chase them away?

There is a large building supply store in our town that plays its jingle and ads non-stop while you shop. It's loud and very repetitive. I find myself wondering why they see the need to play advertising when I'm already in the store! It makes me edgy to the point where I want to quickly get what I came for and get out. I do not tend to linger or look around. The background "music" literally drives me away.

SMELLS

What does the customer smell when they first enter your business? When I enter a restaurant, I want to smell the food—not cigarette smoke! Does your store smell fresh, or does it smell stale, old, or musty? Air quality is becoming more and more important (and noticeable!) to customers. My wife and I do not go to certain places because of poor air quality.

Some successful stores take smell very seriously. Studies have been done on smells as they relate to customer buying habits, and the research indicates shopping habits are affected by what people smell!

THE GREETING

What happens in the moments after a customer walks through your door is of such critical importance, it can not be emphasized enough. The relationship you form with this customer begins right now.

Walking into a restaurant I've been greeted with, "Only one?" That says to me, "Are you a loser?" Just as bad a greeting is, "We close in ten minutes!" Why not start with something unusual and unique, like a smile and a hello!

> *Just when everyone is saying how great you are, that's when you're most vulnerable.*
>
> Walt Disney (1901 – 1966) Founder of the Walt Disney Company

Among the top-ten things customers hate is not being acknowledged when they enter a business establishment. We know this is true. We have all experienced what it feels like to be greeted with a sunny smile versus being ignored, or even worse, treated like we are imposing or interrupting.

One can argue the most important person in the company is *not* the CEO or president, but rather the employee who first greets the customer. For this reason, he/she must be selected very carefully to ensure it is someone with a great attitude, who is friendly and outgoing. It can't be someone who is easily flustered or timid either. The number-one job function of every front-line person is to greet each customer promptly, with a smile, just as you would greet a special guest at home, because that is exactly what each customer is: a guest. A customer is NOT an interruption of our work, but the very reason for it.

The greeting should occur within sixty seconds of a customer walking in your door. Some organizations want it to happen in the first ten seconds. I am not talking about "pouncing" on the customer but simply acknowledging them. Even when you are very busy, any customer walking in should be acknowledged—preferably with a smile and a "Hi, how are you?" or something similar. If you are already with a customer, at least say "Hi" to let the new customer know you or someone else will be with him shortly. If on the phone, make eye contact, raise your eyebrows, nod your head, wave, or do something to let the customer know you are aware of and appreciate his presence and will be with him as soon as the phone call ends. If it is a personal call, it ends NOW. NEVER IGNORE A CUSTOMER. No customer appreciates waiting while the person who is supposed to be serving him conducts personal business.

> *When you go on a diet, the first thing you lose is your sense of humor.*
>
> Unknown

THE CUSTOMER IS THE REASON WE EXIST

I went to a major retailer to exchange an item. I stood at the "Customer Service" counter for at least five minutes while the two employees assigned to the desk complained and argued over some new store policy. Their backs were turned to the counter as they huddled over the new manual, oblivious to the line forming. When one of them finally took notice, she appeared annoyed that customers were interrupting their gripe session. Instead of an exchange, I asked for a refund.

"Terry" at the Holiday Auto Dealership in Austin, Minnesota, acknowledges people waiting in line for service, with a wink and a smile, saying, "I'll be right with you!" They will stand there, impatiently, jingling their keys, but as soon as he acknowledges them, the jingling stops—100% of the time.

Ignoring a customer is costly. Not only might you lose a sale, you could lose a customer forever as well. For example, interested in personal watercraft, I went to a boat dealer a few hours from my home. Looking at the display of Sea-Doos, I stood on the lot for at least fifteen minutes, but when no one came out to help me, I went inside. Two men were standing behind the "Customer Service" counter, but neither acknowledged me. My professional curiosity now piqued, I looked at the brochures and waited. And waited. Then I waited some more. After reading the entire full-color, expensive brochure describing in great detail the exact model I wanted, I left and drove two hours more to another dealer, who earned $9,000 of my business. Does that first dealer know he lost a sale? Does he realize the money he spent on advertising to get me to walk through his door was

> *In Montana, a policeman will pull you over because he is lonely.*
>
> Rich Hall (1954 -) Comedian, writer

wasted? Like most customers, I did not complain - I just went somewhere else.

Besides ignoring a customer, one of the biggest mistakes is to judge or pre-qualify one. A sales manager at a large import dealer tells of a day she asked her salespeople why no one was helping the grubby-looking man looking at the convertibles. They responded, "Look at him! He hasn't got two nickels to rub together!" She went out to talk to the man herself, and within half an hour sold him two Saab convertibles—one for him, the other for his wife. He apologized for his dusty attire, explaining he had just come from the site where he was building their new 14,000-square-foot home on a lake. Her salespeople were chagrined. It was a lesson never to judge a customer.

I recently attended a nationally sponsored seminar that told us, "In the first seven seconds, a customer forms eleven impressions." If that number is anywhere near accurate, it tells us we must manage those all-too-important first impressions better. Seven seconds to form eleven impressions. 7–11. Easy to remember, critical not to forget.

At a workshop I was facilitating, I met a woman who handed me her business card. Her title was "Director of First Impressions." That is exactly what many of us are in our organizations. We determine the customer's first impression. Front-line personnel interact with many more customers on a daily basis than management, so they need to:

- Be friendly, warm and open.
- Greet each customer promptly, with a smile and an offer of assistance.

> *It's only when you look at an ant through a magnifying glass on a sunny day that you realize how often they burst into flames.*
>
> Harry Hill (1964 -) English comedian

- Know the customer is the *reason* the entire company exists.
- Remember the customer is *not* an interruption. Stop chatting, filing, data entry, or whatever "fill" tasks you are assigned. The customer is job #1. People before paperwork!

Congratulations! You've made a great first impression. Things are really clicking. Now, finish it right. Imagine you are Brett Favre, former quarterback of the Green Bay Packers. You've just launched one heck of a pass. Your receiver makes the catch! That's enough, right? Is the play over? No! Now he must run with the ball! You've made the catch with a good first impression, now run with it as far as you can. That means making sure your customer leaves with a positive lasting impression. This is your best guarantee he will return.

How do we do that? How do we create a great lasting impression?

- As you wrap up the transaction, thank the customer for doing business with you, and mean it!
- Always try to do a little something extra at the end to make it a memorable experience. You don't have to do a lot to stand out. Dan Nelson from the Hampton Inn in Rochester, Minnesota, scrapes his customers' windshields every winter morning. When they get to their cars, they're pleasantly surprised by this kind and thoughtful gesture.
- Show you appreciate them by saying, "I look forward to seeing you again soon."
- Follow up after the sale. Contact them periodically

> *It's the abilities, not the disabilities, that count.*
>
> Unknown

throughout the year with things you feel might interest them. It is important this comes off as a well intended service to the customer, not just a way to get back in his pocket.

- Keep in contact with birthday cards, special event notices, newsletters and thank-yous. I once received an anniversary card from Southwest Airlines. On the cover it said, "It is hard to believe it has been a year already..." Inside it continued, "...since you first walked down our aisle." Creative, fun, and memorable!
- Remember the customer the next time she comes in. Remembering their names impresses to no end and makes customers feel very important. Keep notes as to what was purchased, discussed, or other details you can bring up during future encounters. It will WOW them.

And that's what it's all about. Simple, really. Treat each customer like a special guest. Manage those first and lasting impressions. Make customers feel important, and they will reward you by coming back again and again.

There are two ways to live your life. One is as though nothing is a miracle. The other is as though everything is a miracle.

Albert Einstein (1879 – 1955) Theoretical physicist

As the IRS sees it, America is the land of untold wealth.

Unknown

EAGLE EYE VIEW

- First impressions start before the customer ever comes in.
- "7-11" In the first seven seconds, the customer forms eleven impressions.
- A lot of energy and money is spent to get the customer in the door. Front-line people must take the ball from there.
- EAGLES know it is critical each customer is greeted warmly and promptly. This seals the first impression.
- To make a lasting impression, EAGLES make it personal by remembering names, details of purchases or transactions, and customer's important personal data.

EXERCISE 3:1

Visit three businesses or organizations and keep track of your first and last impressions. Make a list of what you experienced. What did you see, feel, smell, touch, and hear? Observe signs, the parking lot, the condition of the building, cleanliness, the furniture and fixtures, and the background noise or music. How did each of these elements make you *feel*? Time how long it took for someone to greet you. What did they say? How was their attitude? How do you feel now? What was your first impression of the business and how long did it take? Write a critique of each place. List both positive and negative experiences. If they need to improve, write how they could create a better first impression. Be specific and detailed. If they made an excellent impression, write down each element that went into creating it. Again, be detailed and specific.

> *Things turn out the best for the people who make the best of the way things turn out.*
>
> John Wooden (1910 -   ) NCAA Hall of fame basketball coach

Compare these lists to what an average customer experiences when doing business with your organization. Are you better or worse? What specifically can you do to improve, and what will you do to make it happen?

EXERCISE 3:2

Think about ways you and your organization can ensure your customer has a great last(ing) impression. What specifically can you do to keep the relationship alive? In what ways can you keep in touch with them? Who will follow up and when?

EXERCISE 3:3

Have every employee (or a large diverse group) visit your facility as a typical customer. Have everyone look at the facility through "fresh eyes," like a new customer might. What stands out and needs attention? What do the signs look like, the parking lot, the paint, or the grounds? What do you need to improve to make it more likely customers begin their experience with a positive first impression?

EXERCISE 3:4

Discuss as a group what your employee "dress code" is. What is appropriate or inappropriate? What is your policy on hair, tattoos, perfumes or colognes, facial hair, earrings, and piercings? How do you enforce it?

In business you get what you want by giving other people what they want.

Alice MacDougall (1867 – 1945) American businesswoman

There is no success without hardship.

Sophocles (495 – 406 BC) Greek tragedian

"Honey, when you say we can't communicate... what exactly do you mean?"

Don't let it end like this.
Tell them I said something.

Last words of Pancho Villa (1878 – 1923) Mexican general

4

Verbal Communication

Nothing is more vital to a positive relationship than good communication. Good communication equals a good relationship. Ask any happily married couple of more than a dozen years what the "secret" to a successful marriage is, and they will tell you the same thing – communication. A survey by *USA Today* asked what percent of divorces are caused by a lack of communication. The survey cited up to 90% as the primary reason. This is a staggering statistic. Do our customers *divorce* us? Sure they do, and many times simply because of the way we communicate–or don't communicate–with them.

Merriam-Webster defines communication as "a process by which information is exchanged between individuals through a common system of symbols, signs, or behavior; personal rapport." Communication tells me what you are thinking, feeling, wanting, and vice-versa. It brings us to *true* understanding. So when we communicate with a customer, we should do so with all of the above in mind. We want to know what our customer is thinking, what she is feeling, what she wants. This helps us understand her and her needs. If we regularly accomplish this, it brings us closer. It helps us form a bond. That bond is the glue holding

> *He can compress the most words into the smallest idea of any man I ever met.*
>
> Abrahan Lincon (1809-1865) 16th U.S. President

the relationship together, and it engenders loyalty. Loyalty cannot be *purchased*—it can only be *earned.*

Right now you are probably thinking, "I speak English; I know how to communicate." Yes you do and that's a good start. To take it to another level however, we need to examine how we use our words and which words we choose.

KEEP IT REAL

Perhaps the most important aspect of good communication is to keep it real. Let's talk to our customers like they are friends. I'm not a fan of the canned speech or scripted greeting for this very reason. While it is appropriate for employees to have *guidelines* for greeting, responding, and talking to customers, it's also wise for them to have the freedom to be flexible enough to put it into a normal mode of speech. For instance, when I walk into Burger King and am greeted with "Hi! Welcome to Burger King, home of the Whopper, where we do it your way! Would you like to try our Mega-Whopper Meal Deal?!" I typically find myself wondering if I'm talking to a robot or a person. When the greeting is monotone or canned, I also question the sincerity of the welcome.

Rote dialog comes across as insincere, defeating our desire and ability to create a relationship with our customer. This builds an artificial wall (you're on that side, I'm on this) instead of a bond. And because it's not real, it is tuned out. It becomes nothing but background noise and is filtered out.

If you've flown on a commercial airline you know exactly what I'm talking about. Airlines are notorious for rote dialog. And what do we do? We ignore their instructions for using our seat bottoms as flotation devices or how the seat belt

> *I wish people who have trouble communicating would just shut up.*
>
> Tom Lehrer (1928 -) Singer, satirist, pianist

buckle works. We disregard the warning to be careful when opening the overhead bins because the contents may have shifted. As a result, we pay no attention when they say, "We do wish to thank you for choosing Generic Airlines for your travel today. We know you have other travel options and we do appreciate you flying with us. If Phoenix is your final destination, we do hope you enjoy your stay." What's wrong with a simple, "Thank you for flying with us, enjoy your day!" Isn't that more like how you talk to a friend?

This brings me to an airline that consistently gets it right. I love flying Southwest Airlines and choose them every chance I get. They treat me like a person and talk to me like a friend. They make me feel comfortable and at ease. They make me laugh, which is probably why I feel at ease. I have collected some terrific lines uttered by the great folks at Southwest Airlines:

- "Do not move to another seat until told to do so by a uniformed crew member. If a nude crew member approaches, disregard!"
- "This is a non-whining, non-complaining flight."
- "If, in the unlikely event, the cabin decompresses, an air mask will drop down from overhead. The first three minutes are free; it is $2.25 per minute after that."
- "The attendants will be checking to make sure your seat belts are fastened, luggage is stowed, hair is combed and teeth are brushed."
- "Smoking is allowed outside on either wing, but they are hard to light. If you can light it, you can smoke it."
- "If this flight should become a cruise, use your seat or

The secret to a good sermon is to have a good beginning and a good ending and having the two as close together as possible.

George Burns (1896 – 1996) Comedian, actor

your neighbor as a flotation device.
- "In case you haven't been in an automobile since 1954, this is a seatbelt."
- "Watch the overhead bins because, as we all know, shift happens!"
- "You do have other choices in airlines... Not better, just other."
- "If you enjoyed your flight, our names are Danielle, Iris, and Linda; if you didn't, our names are Rose, Karen, and Sue, and this is Generic Airlines."

The folks at Southwest Airlines use humor brilliantly. Not only does it relieve what is a tense experience for some, but passengers are far more likely to pay attention to what is being said. That's because they are entertained while being given important information.

Some world-class organizations do use scripts for regular interaction with customers. Many of them have found that the exact words can be altered for personal preferences, but having a script employees can depend on—or fall back on—helps them relax and make the customer experience better.

KEEP IT POSITIVE

McDonalds discovered they could increase soft drink sales—a high margin item—simply by changing how they responded when a customer ordered one. Instead of asking "Small, medium, or large?" when a customer ordered a soft drink they assumed he wanted large and confirmed by asking, "Large one, sir?" In many instances, the customer would respond with a, "Yes," "sure." or "That's fine."

Man does not live by words alone, despite the fact that sometimes he has to eat them.

Adlai Stevenson (1835 – 1914) US Vice President

Keeping it positive you will:

- Use the customer's name.
- Be courteous by using a sincere please, thank you, you're welcome, excuse me, I'm sorry, hello, good morning, good bye, good night, or how are you? and wait for the reply.
- Use phrases like, "It would be my pleasure to…" and "I would be happy to..."
- Replace phrases such as, "No, I can't do that…", "You have to...", and "Your paperwork isn't filled out correctly..." with "What I can do is..." and "Let me help you with that so we can process this quickly for you."

You should avoid:

- "I don't know" or "ya know".
- "No".
- "But…" (ban the But!).
- Profanity and/or slang.
- "I don't care."
- "That's not my job."
- "That's the rule, and I don't make the rules."
- "I didn't do that."
- Gossip.
- Criticism.
- Lying.
- Politics or religion.
- Racial or ethnic references.
- "Because I said that's the way it is."
- "Read the sign."
- "I already told you that!"
- "You don't understand."

> *It is not what you say that counts – it is what they hear and absorb that really matters.*
>
> Red Auerbach (1917 – 2006) Hall of Fame NBA coach

- "You'll have to..."
- "You should have..."
- "That's our policy."
- Technical jargon.
- ACRONYMS customers may not know.
- Complaining about anything!
- Generalities, such as, "I'll get back to you as soon as I can..." (When exactly is that?)
- To be honest with you... (You haven't been honest until now?)
- "I'll let you know."
- "I can't".
- No problem (some organizations feel this is too casual).

WHEN YOU ARE UNABLE TO COMPLY WITH A CUSTOMER REQUEST

- First listen to what the customer wants.
- Show empathy for his request or needs.
- Make sure you understand the situation completely.
- Offer alternatives. Tell him what you CAN do for him.

Make sure you express empathy, caring, and compassion to the customer.

I was about to present a program at a very upscale hotel in Hawaii. The person setting up the conference room spoke very little English. I asked for a wine carafe for a demonstration and his response was, "No problem!" He ran from the room, returning a few minutes later with a water pitcher. I explained I needed a carafe, something with a narrow neck. Again, he said, "No problem! No problem!" and took off for the back room. In a minute he was back with a big

> *You can get much further with a kind word and a gun than you can with a kind word.*
>
> Al Capone (1899 – 1947) Gangster

jar. Again I explained what I needed. He responded with his, "No problem!" and took off. He came back a few minutes later, this time with a wine carafe. I was impressed with his sense of urgency and his attitude to get it done even if it *was* a problem.

AVOID GENERALITIES

Frequently, someone on the phone will ask, "Can you hold for a second?" Is it really a second? No. Give the customer a realistic time estimate and stick to it.

I was in a restaurant where the server kept coming back and telling us our order would "be right out." She came back after forty minutes of this, and said, "It'll be just another minute." I shot back with, "If this minute is as long as the last minute, we are not going to wait." Customers get frustrated when you don't tell them the truth or when you are vague. Don't say, "I'll get right back to you" What does that mean? Your customer may wait by the phone for a response when what you really mean is "within a few days." Might that upset your customer? Be specific and be honest.

INTERNAL CUSTOMER (FELLOW EMPLOYEES) COMMUNICATION

I was invited to a large organization (500+ employees) where the CEO told me employee attitudes were strongly negative and people didn't get along or like each other. I met him the next morning in the reception area. We walked thirty feet to the elevator, went up to the fourth floor, down a long corridor past the employee cafeteria and into the executive offices. We passed no less than a dozen employees along the way. The CEO never once looked at them, acknowledged them or said a thing to any of them. Now where do you think

> *I could not fail to disagree with you less.*
>
> Boris Johnson (1964 -) British Member of Parliament

attitudes start in that workplace? I believe management sets the tone in an organization and must demonstrate the behavior they want to see in employees.

We need to treat our co-workers as well as we treat our best customers. Hal Rosenbluth wrote a great book titled *The Customer Comes Second.* His theory is that we need to take care of each other first and great customer service will automatically follow. We all have tough times, tough days, and even tough lives sometimes. We need to be there for each other! The simple act of greeting one another when we come to work and asking something about the other person shows you know them and you care. It goes a long way toward building a positive work environment.

Disney has a rule that stipulates you will always greet another person you pass with a smile, which includes all guests *and* co-workers. This goes a long way toward improving how we treat each other—and how we feel as a result—by recognizing and acknowledging each others worth!

When it comes to internal customers (co-workers or employees) always remember: *Praise in public, criticize in private*. People usually do more for praise and recognition than for money. Look for ways to *sincerely* praise an internal customer and he/she will be happier all day. If correction or criticism is necessary, do so in private, and as diplomatically as possible. It is important to make sure you convey that the behavior is the problem, not the person. (See *The One Minute Manager* by Kenneth Blanchard, PhD and Spencer Johnson, MD)

Some organizations have a five to ten minute meeting at the start of each shift. It keeps everyone in the loop and can motivate teams to achieve better results. It also gives staff

> *Small talk serves a big purpose.*
>
> Unknown

time to discuss or identify problems or things needing attention. Some studies confirm this to be a highly preferred method of communication for employees.

Mark Twain once remarked "Everyone brightens up a room -- some when they enter and some when they leave!" Think about yourself. Do your co-workers look forward to seeing you each day or do they secretly wish you would call in sick or not come in at all? You have a choice each day to make your co-workers' days better or worse by what you do and how you respond to them. Be someone in the workplace people want to be around -- it makes their day better, and it will surely make your day better too!

SEEK UNDERSTANDING

For any relationship to be successful, the parties involved must know each other. If we wish to have a positive relationship with someone, we must understand him, his wants and needs, and have the desire to help him achieve his goals.

Look at the relationships each of us are fortunate to have in our lives: friends and family. Take a moment to think about two people you care about—one a family member, the other a friend. Focus on these two people. Think about how much you know about them. Feel how much you care for them. You revel in their successes: an "A" on a report card, a home-run in softball, a new tooth, or a job promotion. You want the best things in life for them; if they are happy, you are happy. You help them achieve their goals by taking the kids to practice, paying for college, watching the kids while your spouse goes to class, etc. You are the one they lean on

> *Many attempts to communicate are nullified by saying too much.*
>
> Robert Greenleaf (1904 – 1990) Founder of Center for Applied Ethics

in tough times and you celebrate with them in joyous times. You have great relationships.

GIVE THEM WHAT THEY WANT

Although our relationships with customers won't be as profound or intimate as our relationships with loved ones, we hope they will be meaningful and successful. Understanding what makes our personal relationships work helps us make our professional relationships work, as well. The key word is "understanding." Just as in our personal relationships, the people in our professional relationships—our customers and co-workers—want to be heard and understood. I don't know if there is a greater gift or compliment we can pay to someone than to listen with the goal of understanding his/her wants and needs. Do just that one thing and he/she will come back time and again.

Little more than a century ago, people communicated mainly through writing letters. They were delivered by ship, horse, sled dogs, or on foot, the entire process being very lengthy. Today, technology has given us so many vehicles for communicating: cell phones, fax machines, e-mail, voice mail, and instant messaging. Instead of taking days, weeks, or months to deliver a message, it's all accomplished instantaneously. Sending an e-mail half way around the world is done with the click of a mouse. We speak to each other in sound bites, conducting abbreviated conversations via text messages: "r u @ hm?"

We all yearn to be heard and understood. Observe how many people cannot even drive their car or take a walk without chatting on their cell phones. With all this fabulous communication technology at our disposal, why does it seem

> *It does not require many words to speak the truth.*
>
> Chief Joseph (1840 – 1904) Chief of Wallamwatkain Tribe

we actually communicate *less*? Or perhaps I should say: we *understand* each other less. We talk more but understand less.

Just for fun, here is an example of communication between two people who truly understand each other. Two fishermen:

"Hiyamac"
"Lobuddy"
"Binearlong?"
"Coplours"
"Cetcheny?"
"Goddafew"
"Kindarthay?"
"Bassencarp"
"Ennysizetoom"
"Couplapowns"
"Hittenhard?"
"Sordalike"
"Wachoosen?"
"Gobbawurms"
"Fishanonaboddum?"
"Rydononaboddum"
"Whatchadrinkin?"
"Jugajimbeam"
"Igoddago"
"Tubad"
"Seeyaroun"
"Yeahtakideezy"
"Guluck!"

> *Be sincere, be brief, be seated.*
>
> Franklin D. Roosevelt (1882 – 1945) 32nd U.S. President

LEAVE YOUR EGO AT HOME

When it comes to communicating with customers, we must remember: it's all about *them*, not us. Communication doesn't mean we blabber on and on, trying to impress the customer with our knowledge. Communication doesn't mean we talk because we like to hear ourselves speak. Although good customer service usually involves talking to the customer, it isn't about us *speaking* to the customer, it is about *connecting* with the customer. Salesmen often make this mistake. Because they possess so much knowledge and information about their product, they can pontificate about horsepower, fuel efficiency, aerodynamic capabilities, and safety features. I have witnessed an automobile salesman ply a customer with so much unwanted information about the *performance features* of an SUV, when she was mainly interested in *safety*. He probably thought he was so dazzling with his knowledge, she would just *have to* buy the vehicle from him. Had he listened to her needs instead, he would have found her hot-button issues and not driven her out of the showroom.

Another mistake we make is talking in technical terms or jargon of our particular industry. A landscaper may *think* he impresses his client by saying he is going to plant an "Acer Saccharum" in her yard, when, in fact, he is creating distance between himself and his client. If she doesn't know what an Acer Saccharum is, she more likely ends up feeling stupid. Is this any way to build a relationship? The landscaper suggesting a Sugar Maple is bound to create positive feelings. He is far more likely to get the job and to build a relationship in the process.

The same holds true for industry jargon and acronyms.

> *I never know how much of what I say is true.*
>
> Bette Midler (1945 -) Singer, actress.

Just because you know what it means, don't assume your customer does. That's rude. Let's go back to our car dealership. A salesman understands when a vehicle is described as having "a hole in the roof, AC, and power," but a customer would probably be scratching his head. Talk to him in language he understands: "This vehicle is equipped with a sunroof, air conditioning, power windows, power locks, and power seats."

Our business isn't our sound stage. We must always remember, it's *not* about us. It *is* all about serving our customer. In order to do so we need to focus on the other half of a conversation—the part where *they* speak and *we* listen.

BE IMPECCABLE WITH YOUR WORD

I've saved the most important for last. This statement is from the book *The Four Agreements* by Don Miguel Ruiz, and is actually the first agreement. It blew me away with its brilliant simplicity. If we do just this one thing in our life, be impeccable with our word, everything else will fall into place. As Ruiz points out, it's very simple, yet extremely powerful. He writes, "Regardless of what language you speak, your intent manifests through the word."

We know our "word" is important and weighty. We have our share of sayings that confirm it: "His word is his bond." "You have my word on it." "I give you my word." Why? "Because I said so!"

Our word represents our integrity, honesty and sincerity. We have integrity when we do what we say we will do. When we speak the truth, we are honest. When our feelings

> *He may look like an idiot and talk like*
> *an idiot, but don't let that fool you --*
> *he really is an idiot.*
>
> Groucho Marx (1890 – 1977) Comedian

match what we speak, we are sincere.

We back up our words with action. We do what we say we're going to do. "The package will be there in three days" means the package arrives in three days, not five. "I will credit your account" means the customer should not have to scrutinize his statement to be assured of receiving the credit. A voice mail stating "I will return your call before the end of the day" means you will not leave your office until you have called everyone who left a message. "I will start your remodeling project next Monday" means the customer will hear saws and hammers on Monday morning.

If you always do what you say, you will worry significantly less. Think how much stress you will eliminate from your life! Think how valuable you will be to your customers. They will always be able to count on you. What a reputation you will build!

Remember: the only things certain in this life are death and taxes... and your word.

KEEP THEM INFORMED

Someone once said we need to "over communicate" when it comes to our customers. They want to know how long the wait is going to be, how long it will take to process their loan or repair their dishwasher. A huge issue for hospitals is emergency room waiting time. Patients want to know how long the wait will be, but nobody comes out to tell them. Keep your customers informed especially when you have unexpected delays or changes. That is when it is most important. Anxiety follows closely on the heels of uncertainty. An anxious customer is *never* a satisfied customer.

> *To understand others and be*
> *understood by all, know the big words,*
> *but use the small.*
>
> Unknown

EAGLE EYE VIEW

- EAGLES keep it real. Talk to your customers like real people, like you talk to a friend.
- EAGLES avoid negatives: negative attitudes, rigid thought, excuses, gossip, complaints, and lies.
- EAGLES admit when they are wrong. Don't be afraid to say, "I'm sorry." People are usually willing to forgive.
- EAGLES use humor. It eases tension, focuses attention, makes you likable, and helps others see you as a friend.
- Communicating with internal customers is every bit as important as our communication with external customers.
- EAGLES are specific. They avoid generalities. Tell your customer if it's going to be a thirty-minute wait to be seated. Don't say something vague or untrue like, "I'll seat you shortly."
- EAGLES seek understanding. Every human being wants to be understood. Understanding your customer helps you meet wants and needs.
- EAGLES give them what they want. Offer alternatives if you are unable to do what they want. Tell them what you CAN do.
- EAGLES speak *their* language; avoid acronyms, jargon, slang, and technical terms.
- Your word is your bond. It defines who you are. Are you honest? Do you have integrity? Are you sincere? Do you adhere to the highest ideals?

> *Honest criticism is hard to take, particularly from a relative, a friend, an acquaintance, or a stranger.*
>
> Franklin P. Jones

EXERCISE 4:1

Keep track of all your conversations at home and work for one full day. Write down how many times you find yourself complaining, being negative or confrontational. Record how many times you use words and phrases you should avoid. Be aware and record if you do a majority of the talking or if you let other people talk. Record the times you find yourself not being effective when trying to communicate. What is going wrong? At the end of the day, record what specific ways you can be more effective in communication skills and what you are going to do.

EXERCISE 4:2

Record all interactions with customers when you are unable to do exactly what they want for one full week. What specifically did you say in response and what results did you get? How *do* you say “no” to a customer? Meet as a department or a team and discuss these situations and how to handle them better in the future.

> *The eyes are more exact*
> *witnesses than the ears.*
>
> Heraclitus

EXERCISE 4:3

Analyze your communication with internal customers. Do co-workers have opportunities to discuss problems, share ideas or communicate efficiently with other departments or other shifts? What can you do as an organization to improve communication channels?

EXERCISE 4:4

What can you do as an organization to keep your customers better informed? What action do you need to take to make it happen?

Nothing can stop the man with the right mental attitude from achieving his goal.

Thomas Jefferson (1743 – 1826) 3rd President US

If you promise not to believe everything your child says happens at this school, I'll promise not to believe everything he says happens at home.

English Schoolmaster

Guilt – the gift that keeps on giving.

-Erma Bombeck (1927-1976) Humorist

Life is full of fresh starts.

Unknown

"That's our mission statement. If people follow that, everything else seems to fall into place."

A smile increases your face value.

Dolly Parton in Steel Magnolias (1946 -) Singer, actress

5

Non-Verbal Communication

In my restaurants I have asked literally thousands of customers how their meals were. The one word response I heard more than any other was "fine." What does fine mean? Does it mean it was outstanding? Excellent? No! Most of the time "fine" means it was "acceptable," "I don't want to talk about it," or "just leave me alone." Customers usually don't want to complain and most don't. So if you're not watching for non-verbal clues, you're unaware of most of your unhappy customers *and* losing *a lot* of business!

A customer is roaming around your store looking confused or angry. A customer runs in the front door and frantically looks around for help. A customer does not look happy with something they purchased or a service you provided. These are examples demonstrating the need to be aware of non-verbal communication skills. Identifying and using non-verbal communication, both yours and your customers', is critical to customer service success.

BODY LANGUAGE

These are all examples of non-verbal communication called "body language." According to Wikipedia: "Body language is a broad term for forms of communication using body movements or gestures instead of, or in addition to, sounds,

> *Even I don't wake up looking like Cindy Crawford.*
>
> Cindy Crawford (1966 -   ) Supermodel, actress

verbal language or other forms of communication."

Human beings are social creatures. We cannot live without one another. We are also highly sophisticated communicators. We begin communicating the moment we come into contact with each other. This is accomplished through spoken words, and also by messages we send with our bodies, whether we are conscious of it or not.

In fact, most communication is non-verbal. One research study at UCLA estimated that:

- 55% of communication consists of body language.
- 38% is expressed through tone of voice.
- 7% is communicated through words.

If this is even close to being true, then humans express most of their communications—up to 93%—non-verbally.

Because so much communication occurs subconsciously, Eagles need to be aware of what their bodies are doing to control what they are saying non-verbally. In other words, we want to send the right messages with our speech *and* our actions.

INTUITION

Much of our intuition comes from interpreting body language. The "gut instinct" we have about a person or situation is often formed by interpreting body language.

Why is it important to control our unspoken communication? For one, our body language communicates more strongly, immediately, and more believably than verbal communication. It is the most powerful weapon in our communication arsenal. We've all heard the expressions "Actions speak louder than words" and "A picture is worth a thousand words." Our body language is the "action" and the

> *A guest sees more in one hour than the host sees in a year.*
>
> Polish Proverb

"picture" we show the world. Conclusions are drawn, and judgments formed by those actions, that picture.

Think of two people at a job interview. One candidate looks the interviewer in the eye as she firmly shakes his hand. She sits erect, head and eyes level, with arms relaxed. She smiles and maintains eye contact. Thanking the interviewer for his time, she offers another firm and friendly handshake before leaving.

Candidate number two enters the office timidly, eyes darting. The hand he offers is clammy and limp. He sits, slumped during the interview, nervous, hands fidgeting. His head is slightly bowed. He finds it difficult to look the interviewer in the eye.

Qualifications being equal, which candidate would you hire? What if candidate number two were better qualified than candidate one? Wouldn't you still be inclined to hire the first one? You might not even know why. "I know the second guy is more qualified, but I just like the first one better..."

OFTEN, WORDS ARE INADEQUATE

Non-verbal communication tells us many things about the relationship between people. Often, this is more important than the message we are trying to get across.

Often we feel uncomfortable telling someone how we really feel about him or her. For example, we don't go around proclaiming to customers, "I really like you!" We demonstrate it through our body language. Conversely, a customer may not openly say, "I don't trust you," but the crossed arms, slight frown, and leaning away says you have a barrier to cross.

> *Light travels faster than sound. This is why some people appear bright until you hear them speak.*
>
> Unknown

THE OFFICIAL LANGUAGE OF THE WORLD

Non-verbal communication—body language—is crucial, Eagles! It is the language we all speak, regardless of country of origin. An Eagle is a master at interpreting body language.

Let's look at some examples to help us understand and interpret body language:

Non-verbal action:	**Interpretation:**
Brisk, erect walk	Confidence, enthusiasm
Standing, hands on hips	Readiness, aggression
Arms crossed on chest	Defensiveness
Hand to cheek	Evaluation, thinking
Tapping or drumming fingers	Impatience
Tilted head	Interested
Stroking chin	Trying to decide
Biting nails	Insecurity, nervousness

These are just a few examples. There are many resource books about how to read body language that go well beyond our scope here.

EYE CONTACT

I judge an organization on how "customer friendly" they are by the eye contact I get or don't get when I walk past an employee. The next time you walk down the hall in a hotel or motel, see if the housekeeping staff looks at you and greets you.

Eye contact is one of the most important aspects of dealing with others, especially people we've just met. Maintaining good eye contact shows respect and interest in what they have to say. Keep eye contact around 60 to 70% of the time

> *How can I know what I think till I see what I say?*
>
> E. M. Forster (1921 – 1989) Broadcaster

you're talking. By doing this you won't make other people feel self-conscious. Instead, it gives them a feeling of comfort and genuine warmth in your company. More eye contact than this and you may be viewed as too intense. Any less and you give off a signal that you lack interest in them or their conversation.

Eye contact shows our interest in the other person. Eagles maintain "good" eye contact by looking the other person in the eye and not being shy. Yet they don't intimidate the other person with too much eye contact, which may make the other person uncomfortable.

Eye contact also demonstrates how much self-confidence we have. If we turn our eyes away, or cast them downward, we do not appear self-assured. We seem intimidated. The other person might feel our lack of eye contact is due to disinterest, boredom, or that we are untrustworthy. Not the best way to foster a good relationship!

POSTURE

Posture is the next thing to master. Get your posture right and you'll feel better almost instantly. What is correct posture? *Attentive* is a great start! If you lean over the counter, or have your head in your hand leaning on your desk, you look like you don't care or don't have the energy to care. A good rule of thumb is if the customer is standing, you should also stand. If the customer is sitting, you should sit with him. Not every job allows you to do this, but it does work when you use it.

Your posture should also "square up" with your customer. Face them rather than looking at them over your shoulder, or worse yet, talking to them with your back turned. Facing

> *Who you are speaks so loudly that I can't hear what you are saying.*
>
> Ralph Waldo Emerson (1803 – 1882) American essayist, poet

them tells the customer they're important, and is likely to help build a positive relationship.

We can tell a lot about a person by observing posture. How that person feels about himself and/or his environment is telegraphed by how he holds himself. Someone walking with his head down, shoulders slumped, and making little eye contact is not very interested in his environment or the people in it. I would add that he probably has a poor self-image as well. Compare this image to someone walking erect and making good eye contact. This person communicates that she feels good about herself, her environment and meeting people—she is ready to take on anything!

This brings us to "open" and "closed" body posture. Arms crossed over the chest is a closed position. It can indicate the person is defensive or feels vulnerable. A customer can read this posture as negative, even if you don't mean it that way. Understanding what a person in a closed body position feels helps you approach and deal with him or her more effectively. You know you need to take a gentle, reassuring approach in order to earn trust and confidence.

Someone with an open body posture has arms easily at his sides or behind his back. He stands or sits erect, but in a relaxed manner, head held level. This person is receptive.

GESTURES

Our hands are a great way to communicate when done in a positive way. We need to be aware of our gestures and use them properly.

A wave "hello" when someone enters our place of business makes the recipient feel welcome. Smiling, making eye contact and raising an index finger when someone approaches

> *All those tired of speeding tickets, please raise your right foot!*
>
> Sign entering Quesnel, B.C.

while you are on the phone lets him know you will be with him in a moment. An open hand is warm, inviting and welcoming. Thumbs up says *Yes! Way to go! Attaboy!* Making a circle with thumb and forefinger says okay. A pointed finger can be accusatory; shaken, it can be scolding. And we all know what the middle finger means. (Hint: it does not indicate the person is number one.)

Have you heard the "customer service sigh?" This is when a customer asks for something and the employee lets out a huge sigh! It very clearly communicates to the customer that he is bothering or annoying the employee. Rolling your eyes or shrugging your shoulders communicates the same thing.

All of these negative gestures should be kept out of the workplace. Remember, don't ever give the customer the finger! When asked where an item is, don't point—take them there.

DISTANCE

Distance from others is crucial if you want to give the right signals. Too close can seem pushy or "in your face." Too far away can seem standoffish or "keeping your distance." Neither is what we want. When you're in a group situation, observe how close the people are to each other. Also notice if you move closer to someone and she backs away, you're probably a bit too much in her personal space—her comfort zone.

Understanding body language and the ability to interpret it gives us two advantages:

1. It enables us to project the desired message to our customers and communicate more effectively.

> *Smoking is one of the leading causes of statistics*
>
> Fletcher Knebel (1911 – 1993) American author

2. We are able to "read" our customers better, enabling us to uncover unspoken wants and needs. We will know if they are receptive to us, upset, bored, trying to make up their minds, buying or not buying.

If we want to understand and relate to our customers more effectively, we must become masters of non-verbal communication. Let's look at the other aspects of non-verbal communication.

TOUCH

To be touched is a basic human need. Touch tells someone you care about him/her. A pat on the back gives praise or reassurance. A hand on the shoulder offers support. A hand placed gently on the arm of a customer or co-worker emphasizes your point, creates intimacy and forms a bond. Touch is a very powerful tool, but must be used wisely. Only touch when you have already received signals it is okay to do so. *Never* touch in a suggestive, flirtatious, aggressive or sexual way. Pay attention to how the touch is received. If the person pulls away, then you need to back off. This reaction tells you she is not comfortable with being touched or is not comfortable with you. See how it goes. Pay attention to feedback. Above all, be sincere.

SPEED OF ACTIONS: SLOW MOTION VS. HUSTLE

Along with posture, the speed at which we move reflects our attitude toward ourselves and our job. Lethargy indicates you are either sick and should be home in bed, or you have a "don't give a damn" attitude. Spring in the step and

> *They say such nice things about people at their funerals that it makes me sad that I'm going to miss mine by just a few days.*
>
> Garrison Keillor (1942 -) Author, humorist

quickness of movement says we are enthusiastic, happy and enjoy what we do. It indicates a great attitude. Who would you rather do business with? Eagles moves swiftly and with purpose.

MIRRORING

When you are unsure about your body language, or until you master it, mirroring is a safe mode of non-verbal communication. It means matching your body language to that of the other person. If he stands with hands on hips, you do too. If his hands are in his pockets, so are yours. Don't make it obvious or it may come across as mocking or making fun of them.

A person usually feels comfortable when his actions are mirrored to him. Or, by seeing it reflected, he might realize his body language is closed. This might cause him to change, to relax and open up to you.

SILENCE

Silence can mean many different things. It can mean someone is thinking, confused, agrees or disagrees with what was said. It can also mean they were not paying attention. It can mean they are too angry to talk. So when someone is silent you cannot assume ANYTHING about why. You need to engage them and find out what is going on.

Silence and pauses are important parts of communication. They provide time for thinking and feeling before responding. Silence shows respect. By not jumping in right away or cutting the other person off, we communicate we are interested in what he has to say. We want to make sure he is finished before we respond.

> *Always do sober what you said you'd do drunk.*
> *That will teach you to keep your mouth shut.*
>
> Ernest Hemingway (1899 – 1961) American novelist

Silence can be intimidating or difficult to handle for some people. They find it stressful or embarrassing and blurt out anything to fill the void. In those moments, they sometimes say things they later regret. How often have we asked ourselves, "WHY did I say that?" When we examine the situation, we usually find we blurted something out just to end the silence.

HANDSHAKE

I was doing a workshop in Michigan, and the human resource manager for a large manufacturing firm was present. She told me she makes decisions on hiring or not hiring based on the applicant's handshake. She looks for two specific things: a firm, confident handshake and eye contact. She uses these criteria for both men and women. People make decisions about you based on your handshake alone!

As we previously discussed, first impressions matter greatly. In most circumstances, this first impression occurs when we meet someone and shake hands. Give a good handshake. Don't be wimpy, but don't be a gorilla either. A good rule of thumb (pun intended) is to match the other person's firmness. Placing the web of your hand (between your index finger and thumb) into the recipient's web almost guarantees a good handshake. Keep your hand vertical; it shows you treat the other person as an equal. A palm-down position means you intend to dominate the other person, palm up means you are submissive to them.

DRESS CODE

How we dress and groom ourselves communicates a great deal about how we feel and how we want to be perceived.

> *I've had a perfectly wonderful evening.*
> *But this wasn't it.*
>
> Groucho Marx (1890 – 1977) Comedian

Like it or not, people form opinions about us based on how we look. In the business world, we not only represent ourselves, we represent our company and associates. Eagles know this and put their best selves forward. It is a matter of *respect. Respect for ourselves, the company or business, our associates and our customers.*

So, what are the rules?

- **Don't dress provocatively.** Sex does not belong in the workplace. Unless you work at Hooters, wear your mini-skirts, revealing necklines and tight pants at the club, not at your place of business.
- **Good grooming** is a must. Hair must be washed and brushed, facial hair trimmed or shaved, fingernails clipped and clean. Go easy on the cologne, after-shave, or perfume. Don't MARINATE in it! If you're going to go heavy on anything, let it be mouthwash.
- **Jewelry:** less is more. Yes, it's nice to express individuality—just be practical and don't overdo it. You know you're probably way over the line when you start to rattle when you walk.
- **Clean clothes** can not be over-emphasized. Don't show up looking like you've slept in the clothes you're wearing. With an impeccably clean, ironed shirt and pants, you will look like the best-dressed man in the place. You don't need an expensive wardrobe; a good detergent and iron go a long way.
- **Shoes** are often overlooked by the wearer, but not by the observer. Because we tend to "read" a person from the top down, shoes can easily be neglected. But they speak volumes about a person. Whatever you wear, make sure your shoes are in good condition, clean, polished, and suitable for your job.

> *Try praising your wife, even if it does frighten her at first.*
>
> Billy Sunday (1862 – 1935) Baseball player, evangelist

EAGLE EYE VIEW

- EAGLES recognize most communication is non-verbal.
- EAGLES know actions speak louder than words.
- Body language is our only common language.
- Body language communicates very powerfully and more persuasively than words.
- To be EAGLES, we must become masters of body language; using ours and reading theirs.
- When in doubt, EAGLES mirror.
- EAGLES pay attention to details: eye contact, grooming, posture, gestures, and the speed of actions.

EXERCISE 5:1

Practice reading customer (and co-worker) body language and non-verbal communication for one full day at work. Write down your observations and what you learn.

EXERCISE 5:2

For one full day at work, be aware of YOUR personal non-verbal communication. Ask co-workers what you do that may irritate customers or make you come across as less than professional. Become aware of improvements you can make and make a conscious effort to practice better skills for the rest of the week. Post a reminder or two if you need to stay on track!

Outside of a dog, a book is man's best friend.
Inside of a dog, it's too dark to read.

Groucho Marx (1890 – 1977) Comedian

I will not let anyone walk through my mind
with their dirty feet.

Mahatma Gandhi (1869 – 1948) Spiritual leader of India

EXERCISE 5:3

Practice your handshake with co-workers. Practice being firm (not too firm) and make sure you make eye contact when you shake hands. Make sure your regular handshake is perceived by your co-workers as an example of a great one. In what way can you improve it?

EXERCISE 5:4

At your next employee meeting, greet five co-workers in a positive manner without saying a word. Repeat the activity and greet them non-verbally in a negative way. Discuss your observations with the group on what you liked and what you didn't like.

> *I wasn't kissing her. I was whispering in her mouth.*
>
> Chico Marx (1887 – 1961) Comic actor

The most important thing in communication is to hear what isn't being said.

Peter F. Drucker (1909 – 2005) Author, management related literature

6

Listening & Questioning

When it comes to relating to our customers, there is no greater skill than listening. How better to know and understand our customers' needs than to listen to what they tell us? Developing and using excellent listening and questioning skills is a great way to form a bond with customers.

We used to think the best sales people were the best talkers. (Of course they still think they are.) Studies now indicate the best sales people are the best listeners and questioners. They are able to find out what the needs of the customer are, and fill those needs. People don't like to be sold, but they do like to buy!

Along with listening, we must also be adept at questioning in order to get to the root of matters, to fully understand. Not all customers are forthcoming and direct about what they need or what their concerns are. Some are naturally quiet or shy and some just aren't good communicators. We must know how to ask the right questions to give these customers the service or product they want.

The art and science of asking questions
is the source of all knowledge.

Thomas Berger (1924 -) Novelist

There are two hard and fast rules for listening and questioning:

1. Seek understanding.
2. Respect other perspectives.

We *don't* listen for an opportunity to interject our comments. We *don't* question in order to argue or put down. Our goal is to understand our customers so we can serve them better, to establish a solid bond and to build a lasting relationship.

Virtually all successful customer interactions require listening and questioning skills. Examples include:

- Helping customers in a retail setting.
- Taking orders for merchandise or in a restaurant.
- Conducting real estate transactions.
- Providing professional services (doctors, lawyers, accountants, dentists, etc...).
- Resolving customer complaints.
- Getting customer comments and feedback.
- Finding solutions to workplace challenges.
- Looking for add-on sales opportunities.

In all of these situations, we need to practice active listening: to clarify, seek solutions and to listen for what is *not* said. Too often we talk *at* each other. We think we have something important to say and it makes us feel important when we have the floor.

That's a good reason to listen: to give our customers the

> *How well we communicate is determined not by how well we say things, but how well we are understood.*
>
> Andrew Grove (1936 -) Former CEO of Intel

floor, because it makes them feel as important as they are. How powerful is that? *To make customers feel as important as they are.*

HELPING CUSTOMERS IN A RETAIL SETTING

People who sell cars well know the importance of asking questions to narrow the choices from hundreds—if not thousands—of vehicles, down to the manageable few that meet the wants and needs of the customer. They start with a broad question, the answer to which determines the next question. For example, I enter the showroom of a large, multi-franchised dealer with an inventory of more than a thousand vehicles. Wandering around the lot would take hours, and I still might miss the one vehicle matching all my requirements. This is where a great salesperson is valuable to me, to herself and to her employer. The exchange might go something like this:

> *Hi, how are you today, sir?*
> Terrific, how are you?
> *Happy to be here (smiling and extending her hand). I'm Jane Smith (shaking hands now), and you are...?*
> Joe Constance.
> *Nice to meet you Mr. Constance. How may I be of service today?*
> I'm looking for a vehicle...
> *New or used?*
> New.
> *Car, truck, van, or SUV?*
> I live in the U.P. of Michigan, so I'm thinking SUV.
> *You get a lot of snow, don't you?*

> *Don't question authority – they don't know either.*
>
> Unknown

Tons!
Do you do any off-roading?
Yes, I like to get off the beaten path, do a little fishing, hiking...
What fun! How big of a vehicle are you thinking? Two-door or four?
Four.
How about cargo space?
Yes, I need plenty of space for gear.
How about power? Or is fuel economy a bigger issue for you?
Both—can you accomplish that?
(Smiling) I believe so. How about creature comforts? Are you thinking manual transmission or automatic?

Jane then goes through the list of equipment options, such as air-conditioning, radio/CD player choices, and power accessories. She asks about my concern for safety features, reliability and my desire for sportiness. She finds out my budget and color preferences. By this time she knows a lot about me and how I intend to use this vehicle. She also knows my "hot buttons"—what excites me about a vehicle—and this knowledge will benefit her when she presents a vehicle to me.

Based on the answers I've given, Jane instructs a lot attendant to bring up the vehicle best matching my criteria: a brand new, gleaming black, Toyota Highlander. Cool! Jane Smith has done her job admirably; I don't need to look any further.

Most retail settings don't require as extensive a ques-

> *We hear only half of what is said to us, understand only half of that, believe only half of that, and remember only half of that.*
>
> Mignon McLaughlin (1913 – 1983) Writer

tion and answer process as the car business, but you get the point: ask as many questions as necessary to best determine customer needs or desires.

TAKING ORDERS FOR A PRODUCT OR SERVICE

This may involve fewer questions but is still very important to get right if we want continued business with our customer. In this case, it is about knowing your product. If someone orders an item that is out of stock or back-ordered, know when it will be available. Offer alternatives: "That item is back-ordered. It will be available in three weeks. Otherwise, you might want to consider this item. It is the same quality, similar style and price. Our customers rate it very highly, and it is in stock, available today."

The same holds true in a restaurant setting. If the "special" or other popular menu items are likely to sell out, know how many orders are available before you go to the table to take the order. Be prepared to suggest alternatives. If your restaurant offers wine, beer, or cocktails, know the inventory. Know the characteristics of the wine selection so you can offer suggestions when asked, "What wine do you recommend with this dish?"

Here we go with our questions again:

Do you prefer a dry or sweet wine?
Spicy or fruity?
Do you normally like red or white?
Full-bodied or light?

> *Be a good listener. Your ears will never get you in trouble.*
>
> Frank Tyger

Based on the answers and your knowledge of the wine selection, you are able to say with confidence:

> *For the Chateaubriand, I'd recommend either the Shiraz—it's dry, fat, and peppery—or you could go with the Cabernet Sauvignon. It's less heavy, still quite dry, and complex. Or perhaps you'd prefer the Pinot Noir, which is light and very dry. Any of them would be a great complement to the beef.*

You've just enhanced their experience and sold a bottle of wine—good job!

Often when I am in a restaurant I haven't been to before, I ask my server "what is good?" The response I frequently receive is of no value at all: "Everything!" This does not help me make any decisions. Have some recommendations for your customer. It is important to remember that we make recommendations as a means of serving the customer. If you come across as pushy, using the customer to sell more products, you will lose, *big time*.

REAL ESTATE TRANSACTIONS

Real estate transactions require careful listening and questioning. To those who sell houses for a living, guard against looking at it as just another transaction leading to a commission. For the client, it is likely to be the single most important purchase of his/her life. In some cases, it is the only time this person buys a home. Treat it that way.

> *I hate to advocate drugs, alcohol, violence, or insanity to anyone, but they've always worked for me.*
>
> Hunter S. Thompson (1937 – 2005) Journalist, author

In real estate transactions, questioning is critical to determine buyer needs. Some of the things you need to know in order to best serve your clients are:

- Budget? How much of a down payment do they have? How much per month can they afford or have budgeted?
- Do they have children or plan to have children?
- What size home are they looking for?
- What type of neighborhood do they desire?
- Do they want privacy—a lot of space surrounding them—or the convenience of being near schools, shopping, parks, etc.?
- Do they have pets?
- Do they enjoy doing their own maintenance and/or yard work, or are they looking for little or no maintenance?
- Do they have a home they have to sell before buying a new one?
- Are they "new" people, or are they looking for the character of an older home?
- Do they want to design and build to their specifications?
- Would they prefer something they can just move into, or do they not mind fixing it up?
- What is their time frame? How soon do they want to be in their new home?

These are just some of the key points a good realtor will investigate.

I became a policeman because I wanted to be in a business where the customer is always wrong.

Unknown

PROFESSIONAL SERVICES SUCH AS DOCTORS, LAWYERS, ACCOUNTANTS, DENTISTS, AND FINANCIAL ADVISORS

People who offer professional services want to be aware of how the public might perceive their professions: they are more interested in money than serving their clients/patients. I'm not saying this reputation is deserved or not; I merely point out its existence. It's up to those of us in these professions to change this perception. How? By taking time to listen to our clients/patients, getting to know them, and asking as many questions as necessary to learn how to best address their needs.

I once had a physician, a general practitioner, who asked, "Do you have any questions?" as he turned the handle and walked out of the door. He wasn't my doctor for long. Now, Dr. Huffman spends the first twenty minutes of my appointment peppering me with dozens of questions as he thoroughly completes my examination.

SERVICE

Merriam-Webster defines service as "a contribution to the welfare of others." Sadly, too often in these professions we are more focused on billable minutes than on the people who need and pay for our services.

RESOLVING CUSTOMER COMPLAINTS

This topic is covered extensively in Chapter 12. Here again, listening and questioning are the keys to a win-win resolution.

> *If you do not ask the right questions, you do not get the right answers. A question asked in the right way often points to its own answer. Asking questions is the A-B-C of diagnosis. Only the inquiring mind solves problems.*
>
> Edward Hodnett (1861 - ?)

CUSTOMER COMMENTS AND FEEDBACK

One of the best ways to improve customer service—and thereby our business—is to elicit customer comments and feedback on how well we're doing our job of taking care of them. One way to accomplish this is with comment cards. One of the positive aspects of using them is that people are more likely to be honest when writing anonymously on a comment card. People might not tell their waiter the meal was mediocre, but they will write it on a card. This practice gets responses you might not otherwise receive. The downside is cards are impersonal; they don't help us get closer to our customers. They are also past tense and do not allow us to fix problems in a timely manner, if at all. Customers sometimes wonder (with good reason!) if anyone actually reads them.

PERIODIC SURVEYS

Surveys help us determine if we're improving or slipping. Done on a regular basis and with careful attention to the results and action taken, they can keep our business trending upward. They also help keep the focus on customer service and give us a "baseline" to build upon.

ASKING CUSTOMERS HOW WE'RE DOING

I was checking out in a national chain mega store and the cashier asked if I found everything I was looking for. I told her "No, I didn't find any blank index cards," and she quickly responded with "Oh—that's too bad," and went on to ring up my purchases!

Asking shows we care and that we're interested, but only

> *We must all hang together, or assuredly,*
> *we shall all hang separately.*
>
> Benjamin Franklin (1706 – 1790) Politician, inventor

if we respond properly to what we hear. It also displays confidence. It's like saying, "Hey, I know we're good, so if we have let you down in any way, let's hear it so we can fix it."

I remember being in a family-owned restaurant when the server came to our table a few minutes after bringing us our food. Her question took me by surprise and was indeed memorable. She asked, "Is everything prepared exactly the way you like it?" That was impressive to me!

Customer comment cards, surveys and just plain asking, "How are we doing?" should be coupled with, "How can we improve?"

Menards, a building supply chain based in the Midwest, has a form employees can fill out if they've "Missed a Sale Today." On the form, they identify the item a customer requested that Menards did not have, along with other information and comments. This information goes to decision makers who determine if they want to stock the requested item.

CALLING OUR CUSTOMERS AFTER A SERVICE IS PERFORMED

This is not only a terrific courtesy, it also helps nip potential problems in the bud, before they escalate into major issues. Remember - a dissatisfied customer tells a lot more people than a happy one. The importance of following up after a service? You decide...

One of my best friends recently experienced some fairly serious health problems. Twice he was rushed to the emergency room by ambulance with what health professionals thought were heart attacks. He's undergone months of numerous tests—everything from EKGs and stress tests to an-

> *It is greed to do all the talking but not to want to listen at all.*
>
> Democritus of Abdera (460 B.C. - 370 B.C.) Greek Scholar

giograms and tests for asthma. During the same time period his dog Lucy saw her veterinarian for relatively minor problems: a rash on her stomach, a broken nail, and an itchy ear.

Comparing the two experiences might seem like a joke, except my friend Steve has this to report: Without exception, every time he had a test or procedure, the only follow-up—even for test results—was initiated by him. The various specialists, hospitals, and labs he dealt with only communicated with him when he called them.

Also, without exception, every time Lucy visited her vet, Dr. Tim's office called *the next day* to find out how she was doing. If the situation warranted, she also got a call a week afterward.

Who felt more important and cared for, Lucy or Steve? And they say it's a dog's life! *We wish!*

Feedback communicates more than how you're doing or how we're doing. Feedback tells our customers we care about them and our relationship with them.

FINDING SOLUTIONS TO WORKPLACE CHALLENGES

When dealing with "internal" customers—co-workers and/or employees—our objectives are building a team, solving problems and setting and reaching goals.

To build and maintain a good team: We seek to understand one another by asking questions to know the other person better without prying or being nosy. The objective isn't to gather juicy bits of gossip, but to understand our

> *Wisdom is the reward*
> *for a lifetime of listening...*
> *when you'd have preferred to talk.*
>
> D.J. Kaufman

teammates so we work better together. It's more like a family. We find out a person's strengths and weaknesses so we can best support his efforts, not tear him down. We're building a team in which each player is important.

Look for opportunity: In each of the examples, there exists an opportunity to improve our service to the customer, and thereby improve our business. If, at the end of every encounter with a customer or co-worker, we asked a simple and sincere, "Is there anything else I can do for you?" can you imagine how much more valuable we'd be to that person? What would that do for our business? It's powerful.

THERE'S GOLD IN THEM THAR HILLS!

That declaration started the gold rush of 1849, when thousands and thousands of people poured into California looking to strike it rich. Cities popped up overnight. Many did indeed make their fortunes, but not by panning for gold. There was money to be made by supplying the prospectors with shovels, whisky, or other necessities. Talk about looking for opportunity! Those merchants overlooked the obvious - the gold. Instead, by taking care of the needs of their customers—the prospectors—they made out better.

> *How come I always get blamed for everything I do?*
>
> Dennis the Menace (1951 -   )

EAGLE EYE VIEW

- EAGLES possess excellent listening and questioning skills that help build a bond with customers.
- EAGLES listen and question to seek understanding of—and respect for—the other person's perspective.
- EAGLES practice *active listening*, and listen for the unspoken—what is left unsaid.
- There are limitless situations and circumstances where EAGLE listening and questioning skills are helpful.
- Two of the most important attributes EAGLES possess in listening and questioning are honesty and sincerity.
- Two of the most valuable gifts we can give another human being are our time and attention, and EAGLES do that by listening.

EXERCISE 6:1

Every day for one week, pick one customer (internal or external) and practice asking them questions and listening. Make sure *they* do the majority of the talking. Practice "small talk" and find out some things about them and what they find important. Ask them at least three questions. You can accomplish this in just a few minutes each day, and you will find significant improvements in your relationships when you talk less and listen more!

> *Mothers are fonder than fathers of their children because they are more certain they are their own.*
>
> Aristotle (384 B.C. – 322 B.C.) Greek philosopher

EXERCISE 6:2

Keep a list for one full week of every time a customer asks you for something you do not stock or service you do not offer. Review this list with your team or management at the end of the week and discuss options or ideas you have for offering these products or services in the future.

EXERCISE 6:3

What one idea in this chapter can I use that will have the most positive impact on service to my customers? What is my action plan? What will I do to make the needed change and when?

EXERCISE 6:4

What one idea in this chapter can your organization implement to have the most positive impact on customer service? What changes do you need to implement? When and how will you go about accomplishing them?

Patriotism is supporting your country all the time and the government when it deserves it.

Mark Twain (1835-1910) Humorist, writer

Judge a man by his questions rather than his answers.

Voltaire

There is only one thing as difficult as unscrambling an egg, and that is unspreading a rumor.

Unknown

Listen. Don't explain or justify.

William G. Dyer

I'm desperately trying to figure out why kamikaze pilots wore helmets.

Dave Edison

**"If you'd like to press 1, press 3.
If you'd like to press 3, press 8.
If you'd like to press 8, press 5..."**

Mr. Watson, come here. I want you.

Alexander Graham Bell, speaking the first words transmitted over an "electrical speech machine," which became known as the telephone.

7

Communicating with Technology

Not that long ago—two, maybe three decades—our main avenues of communication were the U.S. Postal Service and Ma Bell (telephone, for those born after the Bell Telephone break up). Technology, especially in the communication arena, has exploded since then. Cell phones are so common that land lines are declining in use. This explosion in communication technology enables us to reach a far broader audience, or market, quickly and easily. And they can also reach us. Or can they?

ENABLE, NOT DISABLE

As long as we use technology to enable customers to reach us, we will be successful. However, when technology becomes an unintentional hurdle or is used as a buffer between our customers and us service quality quickly suffers. The distance between us grows until it is too great to span, and our customers will go where it is easier for them to do business.

CONNECT

It's all about connectivity. Let's look at the ways technology helps us communicate with our customers, and they with us. In each, Eagles look for ways to improve communica-

> *NEVER send an e-mail when angry.*
>
> Joe Constance (1955 -) Entrepreneur

tion—better ways to connect with our customers. We can't have a relationship if we don't connect!

TELEPHONE

Incoming calls—menus: many companies have opted to answer calls with recorded messages requiring the caller to choose from menu options to direct their call. While there is a place for these formats, they are overused.

Companies value the time and money-saving possibilities a menu-driven answering system offers, but Eagles ask, "at what expense?" Are we saving *our* time at the expense of our customers, who end up spending more time waiting and wading through numerous options having nothing to do with their call? We may save company funds by eliminating a receptionist/operator, but our customers end up spending more money on long distance or cell phone charges. People get frustrated when they have to listen to numerous options, only to find their issue doesn't fit into any of them. After pushing several buttons, they must leave a message for some department or person. How many customers do we lose along the way because they hang up in frustration and go elsewhere?

Too often, menu systems routing a caller into voice mail are used as a buffer between our customers and us. What we installed as a cost saving device may cost us much more in lost customers. We can kid ourselves into believing we are saving thousands of dollars in personnel costs, but the cost in terms of lost customers may be incalculable.

Consider this: The person on the telephone is often closer to a buying decision—some studies estimate they could decide within 24 hours—than a customer walking in the

> *My wife made me join a bridge club.*
> *I jump off next Tuesday.*
>
> Rodney Dangerfield (1921 – 2004) Actor, comedian

door. Can we afford to allow that customer to get lost in voice-mail limbo?

I conducted a survey (granted, an unscientific one) where I asked, "When you call a business, would you rather have the phone answered by a live person or a recording?" In almost every instance, a real person was preferred to a recording. Most respondents complained that the recorded menus, while helpful in some instances, are extremely frustrating.

We've all been there:

> "Thank you for calling XYZ. For sales, press 1. For service, press 2. For parts, press 3. For the administrative office, press 4. For all other inquiries, press 5...."
>
> *You press 1 and a new menu starts....*
>
> "For appliances, press 1. For home entertainment, press 2. For car audio, press 3. For computers, press 4. For furniture, press 5...."
>
> *You select 4....*
>
> "I'm sorry; all of our associates are currently helping other customers. Please leave a message or try your call later."

What do you do? Probably call another store. If you do leave a message, you're now stuck waiting by the phone. Will they call back within minutes? Hours? Will you get a call back today? Who knows? The answer wasn't on the menu!

I called Generic Airlines. After picking through the automated menu choices, I actually got a recording that said, "We are unable to take your call right now. Please try back again later." Then they hung up on me!

If you opt for a receptionist in your business or are fortu-

> *If you must cry over spilled milk,*
> *try to condense it.*
>
> Unknown

nate to have one already, here are some phone answering tips:

- **Put on a smile before answering.** I guarantee that smile is felt by your customer on the other end of the line!
- **When you are busy with another customer.** Many times we are faced with multiple demands at the same time such as the phone ringing when we are working with a customer face to face, or we are on the phone with a customer when a customer comes into the store. It seems like a no win situation, and in some ways it is, but there are things you can do to make it less frustrating for you and your customers.

1. If you are helping a customer and the phone rings, continue helping the customer in front of you and let the phone go to an automated system or someone else should be responsible to answer. When there is no one else to answer the phone, the best response is to ask the customer standing in front of you if she would mind if you answer the phone as you are the only one here. Also tell her you will take a quick message and get right back to her. Most customers understand and say yes, some will say no – they are in a hurry. If they say no, it is your obligation to take care of them first and let the phone call go. Most will say it is ok, which means you need to make sure you don't engage the customer on the phone in a long conversation. Tell the caller you are helping another customer, and he can either hold until you finish or you will take his name and number and call him back as soon as you are free. Give him a time estimate of how long that will be. DO NOT do this multiple times when taking care of the same customer. It becomes irritating

I only like two kinds of men
– foreign and domestic.

Mae West (1893 – 1980) Actress, sex symbol

very quickly if you keep answering the phone and the person in front of you is kept waiting again and again. If this happens frequently in your organization, you need to look at changing the system of who answers the phone and how it gets answered when busy with customers. Someone once said that a good employee in a bad system will fail every time. Many times the best answer is to change the system or the way we do things.

2. If you are on the phone and a customer walks in, look at the customer who has physically entered and wave to him by holding up your index finger to let him know that you will be with him as soon as you finish with the customer on the phone. If it is anyone other than a customer on the phone, end the phone conversation immediately!

- **Answer after the second ring.** Some organizations don't want employees answering immediately on the first ring. It doesn't give you or the customer time to get ready. Wait for the second ring and then answer the call. A call should *never* go beyond three rings. Either an automated system should pick it up, or preferably, another person should be designated to answer.
- **Do not sound like a robot if you use a standard greeting.** Worse yet, don't sound like you're bored. Don't rush! The idea isn't to win any speed records by getting through the greeting so you can pass the call on. The objective is to communicate with - and understand why the customer is calling. Remember - *We want to connect*. Example: (smile) "Good morning! Constant Training."

> *Health nuts are going to feel stupid someday,*
> *lying in hospitals dying of nothing.*
>
> Redd Foxx (1922 – 1993) Comedian

- **Introduce yourself to the caller.** "This is Joe..."
- **Get the caller's name when possible.** Often, when he hears you introduce yourself, he will offer his name in response. If not, you might try, "...and you are...?"
- **Offer assistance.** "How may I help you?"
- **Transfer with care!** Every call is precious cargo. Don't drop it! Assure and thank the caller. After he tells you what he wants: "I'll connect you with Rhea right away. If you need to reach her in the future, you can dial her direct line at 249-5555." If the person you are transferring the call to is away from his desk or on another call, let the caller know and give him the **option** of leaving a message on voice mail. Don't just dump the call there. "Mr. Smith, I'm getting a busy signal. Would you like her voice mail, or could I take a message?"
- **Inform the recipient.** Let the person picking up know who the caller is (if you know), and why he is calling.
- **Putting them on hold.** Remember: it is called "hold," not "forget." Ask if it is okay to put her on hold, then WAIT FOR THE ANSWER! Sometimes it may be an emergency. Or it may be a five-second question you can answer immediately and save everyone time. The customer should not be on hold for more than thirty seconds. If you don't have an answer by then, come back on the line, thank her for holding and give her a choice: "Would you like to continue holding—it will probably take another two minutes or so—or would you prefer I take your number and call you back as soon as I have the information?"
  Very few customers like waiting on hold, even though it is necessary at times. Nice music while on hold less-

> *Insanity is hereditary; you can get it from your children.*
>
> Sam Levenson (1911 – 1980) Humorist

ens stress and seems to make time go faster. Some companies run an advertisement or informational message which also occupies time.

Set your phone system to ring after a caller has been holding for more than a preset time. This eliminates forgotten calls. For example, you can set the call-back for thirty seconds. If the caller is still on hold after time elapses, it rings back with a special tone. At that point you (or someone else) pick up to assure the caller she has not been forgotten, that you are working on getting her taken care of, and ask if she would like to continue to hold.

If you place someone on hold in order to transfer a call, let the person to whom you are transferring know who is on the line and the nature of the call, so the caller doesn't have to repeat her story all over again.

- **Remember:** the customer on the phone is not an interruption to our day; he is the REASON for it!
- **Think of it this way:** Imagine the person on the other end of the phone is your boss—the person who signs your paycheck and decides your future in the company. Well guess what? IT IS, and SHE DOES!

There's a great scene in the movie *You've Got Mail* where, by way of apology, Joe Fox—played by Tom Hanks—explains to Kathleen Kelly—played by Meg Ryan—that his putting her out of business was just that; business....

> Joe: It wasn't personal....
>
> Kathleen: What is that supposed to mean? I'm so sick of all that. All it means is that it wasn't personal to **you**, but it was personal to **me**. It's personal to a lot of people. What is so wrong with

> *You appeal to a small, select group of confused people.*
>
> Message in a fortune cookie

being personal anyway? Because whatever else anything is, it ought to begin by being personal!

I couldn't agree more!

If we must use recorded messages and menus, Eagles keep them short and simple, and always give the caller the option to connect with a live person at any time.

Etiquette: Simple, basic manners always make a difference. They include an enthusiastic greeting, giving your name, acknowledging the callers request, asking permission to take the next step and thanking the caller. For example:

Don't:

"ABC Company"
Service department please....
<Click. Silence.>
(Am I on hold or did they hang up on me?)

Do:

"Good morning, ABC Company—this is Ann. How may I help you?"
Hi, Ann, this is Robert Jones, can you transfer me to the service department, please?
"I'd be happy to, Mr. Jones. Can you hold, please, while I connect you?"
Sure.
To the service department: "I'm transferring Robert Jones to you."
To Mr. Jones: "Mr. Jones? I have the service department for you."
(Transfer complete)

Voice mail—recording a message: We don't want to miss any opportunity to serve our customers. For times we

> *I'd rather be a failure at something I enjoy than be a success at something I hate.*
>
> George Burns (1896 – 1996) Comedian, actor

are away from our desk, working with a customer, or on another phone call, voice mail is a life saver. Eagles who use a mechanical answering machine or electronic voice mail use them wisely.

Before recording the message your customers hear, put a smile on your face to ensure your message is warm and upbeat. State your name (so they know they're at the right place) and, if possible, the day and date. When asking them to leave a message, remind them to leave their name and phone number. To eliminate playing phone tag, you might also ask for the best time to call back. Make sure to check your recording on a regular basis to keep it appropriate and up-to-date. (I once called an insurance adjuster whose voice-mail stated he would be on vacation from December 5th through the 12th. I was calling in March.)

Voice-mail—leaving a message: When leaving a voice-mail message, speak clearly and slowly. The person receiving your message is likely writing down the information you provide, so don't rush, especially when leaving your phone number. Spell your name, if the recipient isn't familiar with it. Repeat your phone number. I can't tell you how many people do not receive return calls because they race through their phone numbers like it's some kind of contest to see how fast they can say the digits. Saying the phone number slowly and repeating it ensures the recipient can copy it down, and you are more likely to get a call back. Give a reason for your call so the recipient is prepared when he calls back. Don't leave messages you wouldn't want someone else to hear. (Think mom here.) Some people listen to their messages on speaker-phone. This can be embarrassing

When a man sits with a pretty girl for an hour, it seems like a minute. But let him sit on a hot stove for a minute – then it's longer than any hour. That's relativity!

Albert Einstein (1879 – 1955) Theoretical physicist

for the one leaving the message and for the one receiving it! Be careful. Keep it professional.

Personal calls: As much as companies discourage personal calls, they are a fact of life. Our family and friends need to reach us when we're at work and it's an important matter. Personal calls should be kept short and NEVER continue at the expense of a customer who is waiting (and listening)!

CELL PHONES

More and more we use cell phones for personal use and for communicating with customers. When you use your cell phone for work, *please* be professional! I called someone who gave me their cell phone number and the recorded message was ABSOLUTELY OBNOXIOUS. He obviously wasn't thinking about his *business* customers hearing his message.

Proper etiquette applies to cell phones, too. Don't hold conversations when you disrupt other people or if other people can hear a conversation.

PAGERS

Pagers are great tools. They enable us to be accessible to customers/clients, while giving us control over when to make contact. Unlike a ringing phone that needs to be answered immediately, if your pager goes off at an inconvenient time (when you're in a meeting, or with another client), you can choose to respond at your earliest convenience.

Here are some tips if you wear a pager in your line of work:

- Put your pager number on your business card.

> *He is the richest who is content with the least.*
>
> Socrates (470 – 399 BC) Greek philosopher

- Respond to a page as soon as possible—definitely before the end of the business day
- Set your pager to "vibrate" in situations when an audible alert would be intrusive or annoying, such as meetings, assemblies or when you are with a customer.
- Have an emergency code for family, superiors, or VIP clients to let you know their page requires an immediate response. For example, after typing in their phone number, they can add "9-1-1." Warn them not to "cry wolf." Abusing the emergency system defeats its purpose.
- IMPORTANT: Many times customers can "overhear" what is said on the other end of the line. When you are talking to someone on a pager, BE CAREFUL what you say (Think mom again)!

COMPUTER ETIQUETTE—E-MAIL

All caps: NEVER TYPE E-MAIL MESSAGES IN ALL CAPS. IT'S LIKE SHOUTING! YOU COME ACROSS AS RUDE OR LAZY. EITHER WAY, NOT GOOD!!!

Ahhhh... that's better. It is always appropriate to use formal punctuation and capitalization when sending a business e-mail. It can be acceptable to be more casual when communicating with someone you frequently e-mail, like a co-worker or friend (i.e., not using caps and being somewhat loose with punctuation). It's best to take a cue from the other party and not be the one initiating a more lax form of writing.

Abbreviations: If you're e-mailing a customer, avoid abbreviations, except for those widely known and accept-

> *The most overlooked advantage of owning a computer is that if they foul up there's no law against whacking them around a bit.*
>
> Eric Porterfield

ed. For instance, everyone knows $ (dollar), # (number or pound), and "lb." (pound). But not everyone knows LOL means "laughing out loud," or OMG means "Oh my God." When you're communicating with someone you are very familiar with, and if he/she initiates it, then it's all right to use acronyms and abbreviations. Again, the objective is to communicate, to understand, be understood and to connect. When we use abbreviations, acronyms and terms the other person doesn't know or understand, we have defeated our purpose.

Emoticons: These are cutesy little icons, like smiley faces, added to display emotions such as joy [**:)**], sadness [**:(**], or surprise [**:-o**]. As discussed regarding the uses of all caps and abbreviations, it's probably best to limit emoticons. Never use them when communicating with a customer or client. Use with co-workers is more acceptable, but don't get too carried away—they can be distracting.

Jargon: Along with the communication technology explosion, there has been a corresponding explosion of new words added to our collective vocabulary. Some words, like "navigate" and "text" aren't new, but now have additional meanings. When we use these words, we need to be sure the person on the other end knows and understands their meaning. Otherwise we might come across as a snobby "techie."

Subject line: Make a habit of using the subject line when e-mailing. People who get a high volume of e-mail (like me) often do not open mail with "none" in the subject line. I typically receive over one hundred e-mails a day, and I decide what to open and what to delete based on the subject line. Put what it's about. Not only does this increase the chance your mail gets read, it is also easier for the recipient to refer

> *It may not always be profitable at first for businesses to be online, but it is certainly going to be unprofitable not to be online.*
>
> Esther Dyson (1951 -) Journalist

to it later.

Keep the subject line concise and to the point. For instance: "Confirming appointment," "Price quote," "Meeting schedule," or "Info you requested." Be aware that professional spammers are savvy and use words like "order confirmation" in their subject line to entice you to open it. Knowing this, include some specific information in the subject line to let the recipient know you are legitimate: "Birch flooring shipment," "Part for '98 Rav," "Keen sandal order."

Attachments: When sending attachments it's best to use widely accepted formats for text and photos.

Sending anything to and from a business *must* be kept professional. Only send items relevant to doing business. No off-color jokes, soft porn, funny videos, racial slurs, or sexual innuendo is ever safe. Remember, anything you send or receive may be seen by many others. (Maybe even your mom.)

INTERNET

Website: Does your company have one? Can a customer Google you? If your company is doing business in the 21st Century, you should have a webpage. If the internet isn't used more today than the phone book, it soon will be. Your webpage is your "listing" on the information superhighway. A webpage makes it EASY for customers to reach you. By typing your name or the products/services you offer in the "search" bar, customers from another town, state, or even country can locate you.

How big a deal is that? I'll tell you. I live in a small town

> *The pessimist*
> *sees difficulty in every opportunity.*
> *The optimist*
> *sees opportunity in every difficulty.*
>
> Sir Winston Churchill (1874 – 1965) Prime Minister, UK

in the Upper Peninsula of Michigan. It's more than fairly remote. Yet if you are looking for rugged outdoor or work apparel and type in the word "Carhartt," one of the first sites you are directed to is Getz's Department Store in my home town of Marquette. Thanks to the internet, Getz's is one of the biggest retailers of Carhartt apparel in the world. They ship anywhere and everywhere. Their internet sales far exceed the sales from their retail store. When the sales manager told me this, he laughed, saying, "It's great! I sell more at night when I'm sleeping than I do all day long when I'm working!"

There are a huge number of small independent businesses doing A LOT of business on the internet. Your store hours may be 10 to 5, but you sell 24 hours a day, 365 days a year on the internet. Because of this opportunity, it's also important your website looks sharp and is easy to navigate. Get professional help—it's well worth the investment!

EAGLE EYE VIEW

- EAGLES use technology to be accessible to their customers, unlike ducks, who use it to avoid them.
- EAGLES strive to remove barriers; ducks erect them.
- EAGLES always exercise common sense when it comes to communication technology,
- EAGLES are courteous, polite, and thoughtful when communicating with customers and co-workers.
- EAGLES focus on the relationship.
- EAGLES seek to connect.

> *He who laughs – lasts.*
>
> Mary Pettibone Poole

EXERCISE 7:1

Place calls to several different businesses or organizations that are considered your "competition." Pay close attention to how the phone is answered and how your call is routed. Critique their performance. Take notes on what they did right and the things that made you feel frustrated. Continue until you find at least one company that gets it right—one that makes you feel good.

Next, turn that same critical ear on your own company by placing calls to your place of business. Be objective. How did you stack up? What did your company get right, and where can improvements be made?

EXERCISE 7:2

Get together with your department or staff and discuss communication and technology. Ask for input from everyone about problems they see in using the telephone, computer, and other forms of communication. What things irritate your customers or cause problems for you? What can you do to improve or change? List them, discuss them, come up with possible solutions, and take action to improve.

EXERCISE 7:3

What one idea in this chapter will have the most positive impact on improving service to my customers? What is my action plan? What will I do to make the needed change and when?

EXERCISE 7:4

What one idea in this chapter can your organization implement or use to have the most positive impact on customer service? What changes do you need to implement and when? How will you go about accomplishing them?

**"Yes, I think I have good people skills.
What kind of idiot question is that?"**

Every great business is built on friendship.

James Cash Penney (1875 – 1971) Founder of J. C. Penney's

8

Selling the Relationship

Steve Pelto at Look Realty has been my realtor for thirty years. I have bought and sold more than a dozen homes and commercial properties in that time frame. Other realtors have offered lower rates or "better" deals, but I have a loyalty to Steve. I call him regularly with questions about many things that don't result in a commission for him. He responds instantly, and usually gives me more information than I was looking for or ideas I hadn't even thought of. He calls me when he sees something he thinks might interest me. He has helped me negotiate better deals and is very knowledgeable about real estate and running a small business. I am loyal to Steve because of the relationship we have developed.

The Merriam-Webster Dictionary defines a "transaction" as 1) an exchange or transfer of goods, services or funds and 2) an act, process or instance of transacting. Paraphrasing slightly, Merriam-Webster says a relationship is "a state of affairs existing between those having dealings." For our purposes, a transaction implies one instance of goods or services exchanged for funds. A relationship implies several, or an ongoing exchange.

> *What we see depends mainly on what we look for.*
>
> John Lubbock (1834 – 1913) British statesmen

Unless you are a fly-by-night duck, you are an Eagle who is more interested in the latter: an ongoing, mutually beneficial relationship with your clients. If you are more interested in pocketing the money you get from a single transaction, and don't care about the quality of goods or service delivered, then that is exactly what you will get: money. But maybe—likely—only one time. One transaction. Uno. Forget about growth—can you even sustain your business on one transaction at a time? Or would you rather build and grow through long-term relationships with your clients?

Money aside, which scenario provides the greatest personal satisfaction? (If you think it's scoring the money, then you are in the wrong business. Pardon my jest, but perhaps robbing banks is more in your strike zone.) Seriously, though, if you are reading this book it is because you are interested in the relationships you build with your customers.

You have invested money and energy presenting the right look. Your facility and signs are inviting and represent who you are as a business. You've spent money on advertising, letterhead, and business cards. You've pounded the pavement and networked. You have done all of this in an effort to get people to walk through your doors. Was this huge investment of time, energy, and money all for the sake of one transaction? Heck no! You want and need that customer to come back time and again. It costs A LOT to get him to walk in the door the first time; it costs next to nothing to keep him coming back. And you can lose him if you aren't paying attention.

"Next to nothing" means:

- Making it convenient. Convenient hours, convenient parking.

> *You never really understand a person until you consider things from his point of view.*
>
> Harper Lee (1926 -) American novelist

- Making it friendly. In this increasingly electronic marketplace, people yearn for human contact. They like and prefer to do business with friends. When they consider you a friend, you have a *relationship*. Well done!
- Keeping it consistent. They like what they've received from you in the past and expect the same in the future. The only changes they will accept are ones for the better.
- Don't take them or their business for granted. Don't make the mistake of thinking once you've got them coming back, you can relax your standards. Motivational speaker Jim Rohn warns, "Weeds will take your garden if it is not tended." Customers *always* have other choices.
- Insisting on excellence. From your suppliers, your employees and yourself. To get and keep the best customers, you must deliver the best. Period. We've all heard the saying, "You get as good as you give." If we are not getting what we feel we deserve in our business (or personal) relationships, the first thing we must examine is our own behavior and attitudes.
- Making them feel appreciated and important. Mary Kay Ash, founder of the hugely successful Mary Kay Cosmetics, suggests, "Pretend every single person you meet has a sign around his or her neck that says, 'Make me feel important.' Not only will you succeed in sales, you will succeed in life." Customers keep coming back to the place where they get to feel good.
- Keeping it simple. Make it easy to do business with you.
- Willing to bend. As we all know, relationships sometimes require compromise. You think you are right;

> *The only way to have a friend is to be one.*
>
> Ralph Waldo Emerson (1803 – 1882) American essayist, poet

> she thinks she is right. Both of you have your arms crossed, mouths set firmly. No one is talking. If someone doesn't bend the relationship is over. So you move slightly toward her, she moves toward you, and the next thing you know you're kissing and making up. There are times when we need to give in to a customer to keep receiving their business. For example, a customer thinks the product is defective. Even though it is out of warranty, he thinks he has something coming. He wants it fixed or replaced. He is a long-term customer and has bought a lot of products from you. You have a choice: make him happy by solving the problem or risk losing him as a customer, ending a business relationship.

Human beings are loyal by nature. As a result we dislike change. In other words, if you don't disappoint us, we will be loyal to you. We want to be loyal. Everyone has a favorite restaurant, wants to recommend his mechanic to others, wants to say to another, "This person sold me my house, she'll find the perfect one for you," or "Go see my insurance agent—he'll take good care of you." It makes us feel good—important—to be an authority on something and to help others benefit from our wisdom. We like to think we know who the best attorney is, the best accountant, the best places to eat, where to buy the best sporting goods, and where to get the best deal on a car. My point is, for the most part you don't really need to be mind-blowing extraordinary to maintain a business relationship—just don't blow it! Don't give them a reason to go anywhere else.

I was traveling in Michigan for work and stopped in a

> *Only two things are infinite, the universe and human stupidity, and I'm not sure about the former.*
>
> Albert Einstein (1879 – 1955) Theoretical physicist

small town at a non-chain restaurant. Their lunch special included a sandwich, fries and a drink. I asked the waitress if I could substitute a cup of soup for the French fries, but she said no. I told her I would pay extra, and she still said no. I asked to speak to the manager (who was also the cook and the owner). He came out of the kitchen, crossed his big hairy arms in front of my table and blurted out, "WHAT'S YOUR PROBLEM?" Until that moment, I didn't know I had one! I told him I wanted to substitute a cup of soup for the French fries. He said they couldn't do that for me because then they would have to do it for everyone! I thought it was a good idea, but he didn't. Finally, after arguing with him about his stupid rule, he relented and said these exact words: "Look—I'll do it for you this time but don't expect it again." I wanted to say "don't worry—I'll never be back," but like most customers I just ate, paid my bill, and walked out, vowing never to return. He got my five dollars and a transaction, but he DEFINITELY didn't get the relationship.

To better understand the nature of a relationship, let's look at one of the best types, one that brings us joy and satisfaction: a friendship. How do we become "friends" with someone?

1. You find out his/her name.
2. You discover things about him/her: where he lives, what sports she enjoys, if he likes to fish, what her favorite TV show is.
3. What do you have in common? What conversation topics interest both of you? What makes you both laugh? What do you both enjoy?
4. What are the conversation "hot buttons" that upset your friend?
5. How do you best nurture your friendship?

> *We take fun seriously.*
>
> Southwest Airlines

Let's look at each point and see how it fits into forming relationships with our customers.

Brent Madalinski is one of the best trainers I have worked with and had the benefit of watching. Brent is a relationship expert who immediately gets to know his attendees and works hard at remembering names and other details about them. Audiences and participants love him because he takes the time to get to know and understand them. He connects with people, and he is a very successful presenter because of it.

The name. This may be the most important step. How can you ever expect to have a relationship if you don't even know the name of the person to whom you are trying to relate? You say you're not good at names? Then, it's time to get better. It is a matter of priorities, attention, and focus. Remember, this isn't about YOU—it's about THEM. Anybody—I repeat—*anybody* can become better at remembering names. Here is an acronym I use to help me:

H - HEAR the name.

A - ASSOCIATE it to something.

I - Get an **IMPRESSION** of the person; notice details

R - REPEAT it both silently and out loud.

Y - YEARN to remember it.

Why do you think most people don't remember names?

Never eat more than you can lift.

Miss Piggy (1974 -)

The number-one reason is they didn't actully hear it in the first place. They simply weren't paying attention, so they missed it. Really listen when you meet someone. HEAR the name. You do have to make a concerted effort to master this skill, but it is *soooo* worth it. Act as though receiving and retaining the person's name is like being paid, that possessing someone's name is like getting gold. To a great extent, it's true. The next time you see that person and greet him using his name, he will feel great—important—and you will be elevated in his esteem. It's all about feelings, remember? Make a person feel good, and he is yours!

Some people find it helpful to ASSOCIATE the name with something. It can be their work, an object the name sounds like, or with someone else you know by that name—anything to help anchor that name in your brain. Form a mental picture of the name and the person. The more associations you make and the more outlandish the association, the more likely you will remember the name. Practice with each new person you meet. Have fun with it and you will get better and better as you use it! Pretend that name is gold bullion and mentally see your bank account grow. This tool is guaranteed to work if you use it.

Get an IMPRESSION. Look at the person. Notice details about his eye color, hair (or, in my case, lack of), and features. If you don't look at him, you are much less likely to remember him (remember the importance of eye contact). How many times does someone walk up to another and say, "I remember your name, but I can't place that face!" It doesn't happen. We always remember the face. How often do we remember the name? How many times have we ac-

> *Between two evils, I always pick the one I never tried before.*
>
> Mae West (1893 – 1980) Actress, sex symbol

tually avoided bumping into someone—at the grocery store or a festival—because we are embarrassed about forgetting her name? "I know that woman... oh gosh, what's her name? What is her NAME?" And as we try to will the name into our consciousness, we duck around the corner to avoid an embarrassing encounter. What a shame. Another relationship in peril.

REPEAT the name immediately upon hearing it. Do it silently in your head, then use it in the conversation. The best thing to do is acknowledge it right away after being introduced to someone: "Nice to meet you Sarah..." Using Sarah's name in the conversation not only keeps Sarah's attention, it helps anchor her name in your brain. Ask Sarah questions to keep the conversation going and establish the relationship. "Sarah, do you have any children?" "Sarah, where did you go to school?" "Sarah, do you know..." **DON'T** overuse it -- a few times during the entire conversation is enough. Using her name at the beginning of a question focuses Sarah's attention on you. If you've ever trained a dog, you know that before you give a command, you say the dog's name to get his attention: "Spot, sit!" Besides, people LOVE hearing their name, and they'll like you for using it.

YEARN to remember the name. If you make it your priority, you are more likely to recall and use the person's name. It's about a little effort and a lot of desire.

Remembering names is a skill. Like any skill, it requires practice and patience. Practice. Practice. In the meantime, be bolstered by Confucius, who said, "The shortest pencil is better than the longest memory." Write it down and keep a

Although golf was originally restricted to wealthy Protestants, today it's open to anybody who owns hideous clothing.

Dave Barry (1947 -) Author, humorist

database of customers and other people you want to remember. That way, when they call—even six months later—you can ask about that vacation she talked about. They'll think you're a genius, and you will be when it comes to relationships!

When an Eagle has a relationship with customers he gets to know their likes or dislikes and what is important to them. An Eagle knows if a customer would appreciate a call when the latest fashions come in. She knows which customers to call when there's a sale. If an Eagle has a "techie" customer, he knows this customer appreciates knowing when the latest, leading-edge technology product hits the showroom. If you have a customer who is into old Jeeps, who do you call when one comes in trade? Now, that's having a relationship with your customer!

How important is a relationship with our customers? To answer that question, let's look at the lifetime value of a customer.

A good, loyal customer will be with you for an average of ten years. How much will one customer spend with you over that time frame? To calculate, figure out how much he spends with you in a week (or a month/year), then multiply it by 52 (or 12, or 1), and then by 10 (for the ten-year time frame). A typical restaurant customer easily spends $10,000 in ten years. A grocery store customer spends almost $50,000 in the same store over his lifetime. Car dealerships can reap a $250,000 bonanza from a loyal customer.

And it doesn't stop there. A good, loyal customer will spend freely with you, tell many people about you, come in more frequently, and is more forgiving when mistakes are made. They are easier to deal with.

> *When I was a kid my parents moved a lot,*
> *but I always found them.*
>
> Rodney Dangerfield (1921 – 2004) Actor, comedian

Think about that loyal customer in terms of the relationship versus the short-term transaction. Treat customers like friends, and they will respond by treating you like a friend. Loyal customers go out of their way to ensure your success. They help you improve your business by making suggestions and giving you ideas.

One of my closest friends owns and operates a landscape company in Marquette, Michigan. Steve has an impressive fleet of shiny white trucks. For twenty years he has purchased all of his vehicles—both business and personal—from Public Service Garage in Marquette. On average, he buys a new vehicle every year-and-a-half. He routinely maintains his vehicles every six months, with oil changes every three months or 3,000 miles. If the service department spots a potential problem with any of the vehicles, Steve has it taken care of immediately. Whether purchasing a vehicle or servicing one of his fleet, he never haggles over price. He just asks, "How much should I write the check for?" Steve is a car dealer's dream customer. So how did Public Service Garage earn Steve's business and loyalty? Everyone in the dealership greets him by name. They know Steve's priorities are honest dealings and quick service. If one of his trucks is down, they get it into the shop immediately. If one of his daughters has a problem with her car, he trusts Public Service Garage to treat her with honesty and respect (and send him the bill!). These are the things that are important to Steve. Public Service Garage knows this and, to take care of the relationship, they deliver!

Now let's say the average price Steve paid for a vehicle (estimating conservatively) was $25,000, and over twenty years he purchased twelve vehicles. That equals $300,000 in

> *War does not determine who is right – only who is left.*
>
> Bertrand Russell (1872 – 1970) British philosopher

vehicle sales. He estimates he spends an average of $6,000 per year in the service department. Over twenty years, that adds up to $120,000. By now you've done the math: $420,000, estimating conservatively. Whew! Is that a relationship or a lottery jackpot? Forget buying Powerball tickets—just establish a few more relationships!

Do you think Public Service Garage ever takes a customer like Steve for granted? How many advertising dollars did they spend to get him and keep him as a customer? None. All it took was good service and treating him like a friend. They know what's important to him. They cherish and nurture the relationship.

Knowing the next customer that walks through your door could be a "Steve," are you going to treat him as a transaction, or are you more inclined to establish a relationship?

Here's an interesting tidbit: A Harvard University study found that "satisfied" is not enough. It indicates customers who rates you at "four" out of a possible "five" are *six times* more likely to go somewhere else the next time they want your product or service. It also means a five-out-of-five rating makes them six times more likely to be loyal to you. Is it worth the extra effort?

The point? Make nice with your customers. Get to know them. Small talk serves a big purpose in building relationships and loyalty, which really makes a difference to your bottom line!

Now that we have a good grasp on what a relationship versus a single transaction is, let's look at the quality of the relationship.

For a relationship to be healthy and happy, it must be

> *Reminds me of my safari in Africa. Somebody forgot the corkscrew and for several days we had to live on nothing but food and water.*
>
> W.C. Fields (1880 – 1946) Comedian, actor

mutually beneficial. In other words, it must satisfy and respect both parties' needs.

Notice I said, "in a healthy and happy relationship" and "mutually beneficial." Because here's a concept: the customer is NOT always right. Let's be real—some customers have unrealistic demands or are not as honest as we would like them to be. They might seek to take advantage of us. Are you shocked? In any relationship we can only control and be responsible for our half. The other half belongs to the other person in the relationship. Just as you wouldn't put up with abuse in your personal relationships, neither should you in a professional relationship. You do not have to accept ill treatment.

What is a relationship but a series of transactions? Think about it in terms of your love relationship. Let's say it is one where you "bring home the bacon" and he is home raising the kids. You provide financial support on a daily basis. He nurtures you and your kids for those twenty-four hours. That's a transaction. String those days together into weeks, months, and years, and you have a relationship. And as long as the two of you are happy with the arrangement, the series of transactions, it's a good relationship.

In a business setting, this means the customer gets his needs met by getting good value for his dollar, and the provider makes a fair profit.

For the purpose of our discussion, we're looking at extended relationships with our customers versus a single transaction. As we know, a single transaction is providing goods or service for payment, one time. You hope he thinks the goods or service is worth it so he'll come back. For his part of

> *Why was I with her? She reminds me of you. In fact, she reminds me more of you than you do!*
>
> Groucho Marx (1890 – 1977) Comedian

the relationship, the customer should hope you have made enough money on the transaction to: 1) enable you to stay in business and keep providing same, and 2) that you will want to continue to provide him with said goods or service.

Wait—what was that again? The customer should *want* you to make a profit? Exactly. Where did we get so far off track as consumers to think profit is a dirty word? Not only are you entitled to make a good living providing quality goods and services, you had better be doing so, or you won't be around very long. Are you running a business or charity? If he appreciates what you give him, he should want you to make a profit, which keeps you in business and keeps the relationship going. In a healthy relationship, your customer wants the best for you, and vice-versa.

My point is this: you want good relationships. In order for it to be GOOD, it must be MUTUALLY BENEFICIAL.

We are all familiar with the saying, "Birds of a feather flock together." Since you're an Eagle, your best customers—the ones with whom you have the best relationships—will also be Eagles. So don't concentrate too much effort on ducks. If you can't make them into Eagles, don't be too heartbroken if those ducks waddle off somewhere else.

> *Never doubt that a small group of thoughtful, committed people can change the world. Indeed, it is the only thing that ever has.*
>
> Margaret Mead (1901 – 1978) Anthropologist

EAGLE EYE VIEW

- EAGLES start by learning the customer's name. To remember a name and anchor it in your brain, think HAIRY: Hear/Associate/Impression/Repeat/Yearn.
- Just as EAGLES establish friendships, getting to know your customer ensures a long-lasting relationship.
- EAGLES never forget the value of a good relationship or take it for for granted.
- In order for the relationship to be healthy and happy, it must be mutually beneficial; EAGLES want the best for each other.

People are just about as happy as they make up their minds to be.

Abraham Lincoln (1809 – 1865) 16th U. S. President

Experience is simply the name we give our mistakes.

Oscan Wilde (1854-1900) Irish writer & critic

EXERCISE 8:1

If you take away just one thing from this chapter, none is more important to your success—both professionally and personally—than the ability to remember names. During the next week, practice the skills outlined on remembering names. When introduced to someone new, say the name in your head. Repeat it soon and often, use it in statements like, "Nice to meet you, Jordan…" and in questions such as, "Susan, do your kids go to Lincoln Elementary?" Focus on the prize – the name. See how often you are able to recall the person's name five minutes, an hour, or a day later. The more you practice, the more proficient you will become.

EXERCISE 8:2

Calculate the value of a ten-year relationship with a single customer. Depending on your business or profession, take the average customer, calculate how much he/she spends with you every day/week/month/ or year. Multiply by ten. Treat every person who walks through your door accordingly. Who knows? He could be Steve.

EXERCISE 8:3

What one idea in this chapter would have the most positive impact on service to my customers? What is my action plan? What will I do to make the needed change, and when?

EXERCISE 8:4

What one idea in this chapter can your organization implement or use to have the most positive impact on customer service? What changes do you need to implement and when? How will you go about accomplishing them?

"You're right, I owe my success to luck! I'm lucky that my alarm clock rings at 5:00 AM so I can work 12 hours a day. I'm lucky that my car has a stereo so I can listen to self-improvement tapes while I commute. I'm lucky that my street is paved so I can run three times a week. I'm lucky that...."

If you are positive,
you are on your way.
If you are negative,
you are in the way.

Unknown

9

Attitude and Enthusiasm

Two of the best examples of customer service Eagles are my best friend Rock and his wife Jean. Rock wakes up happy and stays that way all day long. He has a positive attitude that makes me jealous, his positive attitude is truly natural. What a gift that is, most of us have to work at keeping our attitudes positive! Rock and Jean own several Subway restaurants. When you walk in and Jean is working, the enthusiasm and customer service are top-notch. She can be working on three different problems at the same time and still make sure the customer walking through the door gets terrific service, with enthusiasm.

There is nothing more critical to success than attitude and its sister, enthusiasm. Attitude and enthusiasm are everything. I am convinced that attitude is more important than talent, more important than intelligence and more important than education. Best of all, it's yours for the taking. No matter what mean circumstances you were born into, a terrific attitude can propel you into a wonderful life. There are millions of personal stories out there to prove it. Why not be one yourself.

Conversely, no matter how rich, pretty, intelligent, tal-

> *If you have zest and enthusiasm you attract zest and enthusiasm. Life does give back in kind.*
>
> Dr. Norman Vincent Peale (1898 - 1993) Preacher and author

ented, or well educated you are, people will avoid you if you have a lousy attitude.

I could talk and talk about the importance of attitude and enthusiasm, but looking at them in action is far more powerful. To see the power of attitude on our lives, let's look at a few people you may have already heard about.

Daniel "Rudy" Ruettiger: Rudy grew up as one of fourteen children in a middle-class family. "My dad worked three jobs just to put food on the table," he said. But young Rudy was a dreamer. "You're a little boy thinking you could be anybody, you can do anything, go anywhere." If I could go to Notre Dame, I could be somebody. That's the power of the dream. Over and over in school, Rudy was put down and made fun of, even by teachers. He was called "slow" and "stupid." In high school, he was told, "You don't have the grades even to go to community college." But Rudy dreamed of going to Notre Dame and playing football for the Fighting Irish despite being 5'6" and weighing a measly 165 pounds. Through persistence and belief in his dream, Rudy made it into Holy Cross Junior College. After two years at Holy Cross and three rejections to study at the University of Notre Dame, Ruettiger finally made it into his dream school. He fought to get a spot on the practice squad, where he regularly took a pounding and was injured many times. In the final play of Rudy's senior season, with the crowd calling *Rudy! Rudy!* coach Dan Divine put Ruettiger in the game. The much-loved player sacked Georgia Tech's quarterback and was carried off the field by his teammates.

Among many awards, Rudy was given an Honorary Doc-

> *There is real magic in enthusiasm. It spells the difference between mediocrity and accomplishment.*
>
> Dr. Norman Vincent Peale (1898 - 1993) Preacher and author

Wikipedia.org, http://en.wikipedia.org/wiki/Rudy_Ruettiger and http://rudyinternational. Com torate from Holy Cross College and a Distinguished American Award. If you haven't seen the movie *Rudy*, I urge you to rent it.

Lance Armstrong: He's famous for winning the Tour de France a record seven consecutive times from 1999-2005. These record-breaking feats were accomplished several years after surgery and extensive chemotherapy in 1996 to treat testicular cancer that had metastasized to his brain and lungs. One doctor said Armstrong's chances of survival were 3%. The standard chemotherapy for his cancer would have meant the end of his cycling career, because a known side effect was a dramatic reduction in lung function. He opted for a more severe treatment that was less likely to result in lung damage.

While in remission Armstrong resumed training and eventually returned to competition. His domination of the event prompted many Americans to nickname the race "Tour de Lance." In 2002, "Sports Illustrated" named him Sportsman of the Year. Armstrong was named Associated Press Male Athlete of the Year for 2002, 2003, 2004, and 2005. He received ESPN's ESPY Award for Best Male Athlete in 2003, 2004, 2005, and 2006. His yellow "Livestrong" bracelets are everywhere.

Wilma Rudolf: Wilma Rudolph was the twentieth of twenty-two children of Ed and Blanche Rudolph. They were honest, hard-working people, but very poor. Ed worked as a railroad porter and handyman, and Blanch did cooking, laundry and housecleaning for wealthy white families.

> *The worst illness there is,*
> *is a hardening of the attitude.*
>
> Zig Ziglar (1926 -) Author, salesperson, speaker

Wilma was born prematurely and weighed only 4.5 pounds. Though sickly, she was not permitted care at the local hospital, which was for whites only. Over the next few years, Blanche nursed her tiny daughter through one illness after another: measles, mumps, scarlet fever, chicken pox and double pneumonia. When Wilma's left foot and leg became weak and deformed, Blanche and Ed were informed their daughter had polio, which at that time had no cure. They were told she would never walk.

But Blanche would not give up on her daughter. Twice a week for the next two years, Blanche took Wilma fifty miles to Nashville to be treated at Meharry Hospital. After those two years, Wilma was able to walk with a leg brace. Blanche learned how to do physical therapy with Wilma at home, and her brothers and sisters helped, too. The entire family encouraged her to walk. Miraculously, by age twelve Wilma could walk without the aid of a brace. It was at that point in her life Wilma decided to become an athlete.

In high school she became a basketball star, setting state records for scoring and leading her team to a state championship. Then she decided to go out for track. She finished dead last in her first race and next to last in her second race. Undaunted, she eventually became a track star, going to her first Olympics at age 16, where she won a bronze medal in the 4x4 relay. In the 1960 Rome Olympics, Wilma became the first American woman to win three gold medals, winning the 100-meter dash, the 200-meter dash, and running anchor on the 400-meter relay. She was the fastest woman in the world.

> *You will do foolish things, but do them with enthusiasm.*
>
> Collette (1873 – 1954) French novelist

*Women in History. Wilma Rudolph biography. Lakewood Public Library. <http://www.lkwdpl.org/wihohio/rudo-wil.htm>.

Among numerous awards, Wilma was inducted into the Black Sports Hall of Fame in 1980, and the U.S. Olympic Hall of Fame in 1983.

Finally—just to drive the point home—what would *your* attitude be if this were you:

- Mother died when you were nine.
- Dropped out of grade school.
- Very homely in appearance.
- Failed in business at age of 21.
- Nervous breakdown at age 27.
- Took fifteen years to pay off old bills.
- Unhappy marriage.
- Ran for House of Representatives. Lost. Twice.
- Ran for Senate. Lost. Twice.
- Delivered a speech to an indifferent audience. Posthumously that speech would be considered one of the best in history.
- Attacked by the press and despised by half of the country.

Who would blame you for having a defeatist attitude and quitting? Good thing for America this man didn't. He held the country together during a brutal civil war, abolished slavery and freed African Americans. Despite all that went against him, people all over the world have been inspired by the awkward, rumpled man who signed his name simply, "A. Lincoln." Lincoln is considered one of the truly great American Presidents.

More than any other characteristic one can possess, the one most crucial to success is enthusiasm. Dale Carnegie

> *What lies behind us and what lies before us are tiny matters compared to what lies within us.*
>
> Ralph Waldo Emerson (1803 – 1882) Essayist, poet

called enthusiasm "the greatest secret to success on earth!"

My wife and I went to a little restaurant in Nikolaevsk, Alaska for a quick lunch. The Russian woman who owned the establishment was so enthusiastic about her products that by the time we left we had spent $80 for lunch, including an appetizer, dessert, and a box of tea. We walked out, pleasantly stuffed and with a photo of our happy experience (that we paid $10 for!). I think she is the best salesperson I ever met!

Enthusiasm and attitude are contagious. If you are an enthusiastic person, someone with a positive attitude, people want to be near you. They long to catch some of the magic you possess. You never lack for friends; your biggest challenge is finding enough time for all of them!

Conversely, have you noticed people with negative attitudes, people who are always down and want to bring you down too? They say "misery loves company." How true with negative people. Not only are they mired in their own negativity, nothing satisfies them more than dragging you down into the mud with them.

It's called "crab bucket mentality." Commercial fishermen have told stories for years about a fascinating phenomenon with crab fishing. They put a bucket with bait on the ocean floor. Crabs crawl in after the food. When the food is gone, some crabs try to crawl up and out of the bucket. The others, content in their prison, pull the freedom seeker back down. If he persists in trying to escape, they actually pull his legs off. This is crab bucket mentality. Think of this the next time someone tries to bring you down.

A man is driving across the Mackinaw Bridge when he sees a car stopped right in the lane of traffic at the highest

> *Every day is a sunny day when your head is above the clouds.*
>
> Joe Constance (1955 -) Entrepreneur

point of the bridge. He notices there is no one in the vehicle. He then spots a man standing on the other side of the guard rail, looking down at the water. He's going to jump! The man slams on his brakes, jumps out, and yells, "Stop! I won't stop you if you want to jump, but let's just sit and talk about it." They talk for five minutes, ten, twenty... and half an hour goes by. Finally they get up, shake hands, and both jump! (Attitudes are contagious, aren't they?)

Where is enthusiasm lost? We were all born with it, as you see in children. But as we grow we are told "no" so often, we are made to conform. We fear being scolded by our parents (on whom we depend for our survival), we learn to avoid criticism and judgment, and our youthful enthusiasm diminishes.

The death of enthusiasm is tragic, indeed. Enthusiasm sells. Enthusiasm changes the hearts and minds of men, drives progress, invents new medicines and technology and forms civilizations. How far would the American Revolution have gotten without enthusiasm?

Back in the late 1800s a reporter was dispatched to check on the progress of an eccentric inventor named Thomas Edison, already famous for inventing the phonograph. Edison was working on a low-cost replacement for the gas lamp. Seeking the right filament for his "light bulb," Edison had experimented with thousands of materials. To that point, none had the right combination of illumination and longevity. The reporter asked Edison, "How does it feel to have failed ten thousand times?" The brilliant inventor responded, "Young man, I haven't failed at all. I have successfully eliminated ten thousand materials that won't work." Edison's attitude and enthusiasm have illuminated the world!

> *My greatest fear is that I will die before*
> *I learn how to live.*
>
> Henry David Thoreau (1817 – 1862) Author, naturalist

Attitude and enthusiasm are directly connected to self-image. How good we feel about ourselves is reflected in our attitude, and enthusiasm (or lack of it) is the result. The positive person likes himself and presents a cheerful attitude to the world. As a result, he attracts more friends, more happiness and more good things in his life. He likes himself even more, attracting more people and good things and happiness... It's an amazing upward spiral!

On the other hand, the negative person dislikes herself. She thinks, "Nobody likes me because I'm not pretty enough, not thin enough. I don't have any friends. Nothing goes right for me." Mired in self-pity and loathing, she presents a bitter attitude to the world, like the universe owes her something. Consequently, she drives people away, repelling the very people who can add joy to her life. The more people reject her (they are actually rejecting her *attitude*), the more she is convinced nobody likes her. She feels justified—righteous even—in her bitterness. "See? What's the use in trying, nobody likes me." She becomes even more negative, driving away more people and adding to her misery. She blames everyone else; nothing is ever her fault. More bitterness, more rejection, more misery... it's a hideous downward spiral.

The good news is, she can change the direction of the spiral by changing her attitude. Just like Dorothy and her ruby slippers in *The Wizard of Oz*, she carries the ability to go "home" with her at all times.

How do we get and maintain a positive attitude and nurture an enthusiastic spirit? Here are some tips, but find whatever works for you.

- **Be grateful.** Keep a list of everything in your life you are thankful for. It can be a mental list, but if

> *You will be fired with enthusiasm, or you will be fired with enthusiasm.*
>
> Vince Lombardi (1913 – 1970) Coach Green Bay Packers

you write it out, you'll be amazed at how long it is. Too often we focus our attention on the problems or challenges in our lives—the squeaky wheel gets the grease—and take for granted the many incredible blessings we have. When we focus on what we have versus what we don't have, we see the bounty we have been given. We are able to go through our day with a thankful heart.

- **Notice the beauty around you**. Admire the sunrise as you drive to work. Be awed by a sunset, the smile on your child's face, a winter snowfall. If you look for it, beauty is everywhere, and it's there just for your pleasure. We possess the greatest collection of art in the world—and it's free! We just need to open our eyes to appreciate it.
- **Use affirmations daily**. If we don't think highly of ourselves, how can we expect anyone else to? Every morning or anytime you need a pick-me-up, remind yourself of what you're good at or what you want to be good at. Keep the affirmations positive and in the present tense. For example: *I love my job. My customers appreciate my product knowledge. I have a knack for remembering names. I take excellent care of my customers. People really respond well to me. I enjoy meeting new people. I have boundless energy. I like myself!*
- **Set goals.** Know what you are striving for. Measure your progress against benchmarks. Nothing feels better than reaching progressive milestones and achieving your goals!
- **Define your priorities.** Too often we get caught up putting out fires or expending energy unproductively. Start each day with a clear picture of your priorities.

> *You don't have to be sick*
> *to get better.*
>
> Dr. Wayne Dyer (1940 -) Writer, self help advocate

Check yourself at regular intervals to stay on track.

- **Know the reasons you do what you do.** What are you working for? To provide for your family? Put your son through college? Buy a house for your mother? A vacation in Fiji? A cabin in the mountains? To retire comfortably? The reasons we work and strive are as individual as we are. Do we understand those reasons, or are we just going through the motions because it's what's expected of us? Whatever it is that drives you to succeed, remind yourself of it on a daily basis. Keep a photograph of "it" on your desk or taped to your dashboard. That way, when things get tough, you will be bolstered by focusing on the reasons you work. "I can handle anything to put my daughter through medical school."
- **Read to improve.** Your mind is the best asset you possess. Just like taking your car in for oil changes and tune-ups, feed your mind with a diet of good stuff—trade magazines, self-help books, literature... Not only do you gain product knowledge, learn new processes, pick up ideas and get motivated, you become conversant on a wide range of topics.
- **Listen to motivational speakers**. They can inspire, refresh, teach, and give you good tools. There's a reason they're called *motivational!*
- **Be inspired by others.** Learn from the wisdom of others. Stand on their shoulders. I love inspirational quotes (as you may have noticed). They are available online, or you can have one sent everyday to your e-mail address [worldofquotes.com, yourinspiration@famous-quotes-quotations.com, thinkexist.com] The wisdom of the ages is yours for the taking!
- **Pay compliments.** Nothing feels better than making

> *If you want your dreams to come true,*
> *you will have to wake up.*
>
> Joe Constance (1955 -) Entrepreneur

someone else—a co-worker, friend, customer, family member—feel good. Start with those at home. Find something nice to say before you leave in the morning. *You look nice today. That breakfast was delicious—thank you! You are such a smart kid! I'm so proud of you!* No one knows with certainty what the day will bring. I'm not trying to be morbid, but you never know when it will be the last time you see each other. Do the same with people you encounter today, your mom, your receptionist, the guy at the gas station, the woman at the dry cleaners, whomever. Putting a smile on their faces puts a smile on ours.

- **Look for the good** in every situation, every encounter, every person. "As ye seek, so shall ye find." That means what you look for, you find.
- **Take good care of yourself** by getting enough rest, exercise, proper diet and FUN. It's almost impossible to have a negative attitude when you're having fun.
- **Dress well.** Clothes do make the man (or woman). When we look good, we feel good. No matter what your budget, your clothes should be clean and ironed, shoes clean and polished.
- **Be well groomed.** When we make a good impression, people respond well to us; when people respond positively, we feel great!
- **Act with integrity** and problems will be few. For those problems that do present themselves, the solutions will come easier. When we act with integrity, we are in the right—we do the right thing. We earn the trust of others.
- **Always do your best.** When we always do our best, we have little to worry about. We stay out of trouble.

> *It is our attitude at the beginning of a difficult task which more than anything else will affect its successful outcome.*
>
> William James (1842 – 1910) Harvard Psychologist

We don't create chaos. We go about our day with the calm confidence of knowing we perform to the best of our ability. Calm confidence—now that's positive!

- **Speak well** of your organization and coworkers. Ducks engage in gossip and back-biting. Eagles are above that.
- **Be in control** of your moods. Avoid defensiveness and anger. At times we may suffer from contact overload syndrome, too much customer contact over a period of time. If that happens, or you find your mood slipping to the dark side, take a time out—just as you take a bathroom break when nature calls. Soar with your fellow Eagles. Do not spiral down to the depths with the ducks.
- **Compartmentalize.** Keep things where they belong. Domestic challenges stay at home, business issues are left behind at the end of the work day. Don't let a difficult customer affect how you approach and handle the next one. They are two different people!

Positive attitudes include: being warm, confident, helpful, relaxed, resourceful, engaging, welcoming, interested, tolerant, understanding and empathetic.

Harmful, negative attitudes include: being sarcastic, impatient, bored, vengeful, rude, suspicious, stressed out, burned out, complaining, whining, short or curt, hurried, angry and spiteful.

It is more important to be the right person than it is to find the right person.

Zig Ziglar (1926 -) Author, salesperson, speaker

EAGLE EYE VIEW

- EAGLES know that a positive attitude and enthusiasm are critical to our success.
- No matter how meager your circumstances, a positive attitude will improve them. No matter how rich your circumstances, a poor attitude negates them.
- EAGLES observe. Examples of attitude are all around us.
- EAGLES don't let the "crabs" pull them down.
- EAGLES are in control of their attitudes.
- EAGLES share their enthusiasm with others.

Ability is what you're capable of doing. Motivation determines what you do. Attitude determines how well you do it.

Lou Holtz (1937 -) Coach, author and speaker

It's hard to be funny when you have to be clean.

Mae West (1893 – 1980) Actress, sex symbol

We must become the change we want to see.

Mahatma Gandhi (1869-1948) Political & spiritual leader

If you obey all the rules, you miss all the fun.

Katherine Hepburn (1907 – 2003) Actress

EXERCISE 9:1

Your energy level, enthusiasm or attitude just aren't where they need to be. What can and will you do to "pick it up"?

EXERCISE 9:2

This is a fun activity to help your awareness of attitudes and enthusiasm (or lack of it) in the workplace. For the next week, mentally review every employee you encounter each time you encounter them. Do they have a positive attitude and are they enthusiastic, or are they negative and moping? If you catch each other not being positive and upbeat, give the other person a quick, duck-like "quack." It will be a funny reminder to each other and increases awareness of the need to improve.

EXERCISE 9:3

You have a co-worker with a negative attitude or who is usually whining about something. What can you do to have a positive impact on him or her?

EXERCISE 9:4

Make up a list of accomplishments or awards you have received. List everything you are proud of in your life. This is your success file. Keep track of successes you have, and when you have some setback or are getting down on yourself, pick up your file to remind yourself how good you really are.

> *I take nothing for granted. I now have only good days, or great days.*
>
> Lance Armstrong (1971 -) Cyclist

An optimist may see a light where there is none, but why must the pessimist always run to blow it out?

Michel de Saint-Pierre (1916 - 1987) Writer

None are so old as those who have outlived enthusiasm.

Henry David Thoreau (1817 - 1862) Author

Catch on fire with enthusiasm and people will come for miles to watch you burn.

John Wesley (1703 - 1791) Anglican Minister

A mediocre idea that generates enthusiasm will go further than a great idea that inspires no one.

Mary Kay Ash (1918 - 2001) Business woman

It's kind of fun to do the impossible.

Walt Disney (1901 – 1966) Entrepreneur, visionary

"Thank you for calling Customer Service.
If you're calm and rational, press 1.
If you're a whiner, press 2.
If you're a hot head, press 3...."

Make it difficult
to be difficult.

Unknown

In the service business, there is no such
thing as after hours.

Carl Sewell – Entrepreneur & author

10

Policies & Procedures

I was a six-year customer of a telecommunications company where the auto-debit from my checking account for my monthly bill was more than $100. This was for my car phone, which I used regularly for business and personal use. I had an external antenna for better reception. After five years I bought a new car and installed a new antenna. Within a few months, the glue on the rubber pad weakened, making the antenna fall off regularly. I went back to the company and told them of my problem. They said I must not have installed it correctly and would have to pay $4 for another sticky pad. I argued about the defect in the product, but they would not replace it. I even asked for the branch manager, who told me they have not had this problem before and they could not just "give" me the new pad. I reminded him I had been a customer for years and spent more than $100 monthly on my bill. He did not budge. I paid the $4 for the pad and fixed my antenna.

After a few weeks the antenna fell off again. At that point I was not a happy camper and returned to voice my dissatisfaction. This time they told me they didn't carry just the pad and I would have to purchase a whole new antenna

> *Don't worry about what is best for the company, worry about what is best for the customer.*
>
> Gary Comer – Founder of Lands End

assembly unit for $19.95. I wanted to tell them where they could put their antenna unit, but, like most customers, I didn't. I quietly walked out the door, cancelled my service and moved to another company. They lost a customer who would have spent more than $12,000 over ten years because they would not give me a sticky pad that probably cost them twenty-five cents. This is the *same* company that regularly spends THOUSANDS of dollars advertising each month for new customers! Doesn't make sense, does it?!

It never ceases to amaze me how frequently organizations and businesses who are trying hard to compete and win in the marketplace continually upset their customers with stupid policies, procedures, and poorly designed systems. I wish I could say the above instance is rare, but it isn't. Too many companies have ridiculous policies that serve nothing more than to irritate their best customers.

Here are a few more examples to drive the point home:

- We were in a national fast food chicken franchise and decided to eat in the dining room. The loud music being played was absolutely annoying everyone in our group. We asked to have the music turned down but didn't notice any change. We returned to ask again and were told they *had* turned it down (still imperceptible to us). The *third* time we complained we were told the employees liked the loud music. We left and have never been back.
- An acquaintance told me of buying a new motorcycle costing more than $9,000, only to find it missing an attachment bolt and nut on the windshield assembly. He returned to the dealer and was told he would have to buy a new assembly unit for $179. They did not sell just the bolt. He argued that because it was a new

> *Heroic service does not come from policy manuals. It comes from people who care.*
>
> Disney University

bike they should give it to him. He ended up leaving, swearing he would never buy another thing from that dealer. (He eventually found exactly what he needed at a hardware store for less than $1!)

- I was standing outside a bagel shop on a freezing February morning in Minneapolis. The time was 5:54 a.m. I was not the only customer waiting for the shop to open at 6:00 a.m. We could see employees were busy inside the shop, so we banged on the door for them to let us wait inside until they opened. An employee came to the door, showed me his watch, and said they opened in five minutes. He then continued with his pre-opening duties with the door locked.
- I'm in my hometown national-chain office supply store a few times every week. Most of the employees know me by name and use it frequently, to my delight. The assistant manager, however, would rather follow company policy than provide great service. Every time he's at the counter ringing out my purchases he calls me "sir." I told him on numerous occasions I didn't like to be referred to as "sir," and to please call me Joe. He kept calling me sir. Every single time I'm in there he asks for my ID (again, a company policy that irritates the best customers), even though he and all the other employees know me. Finally, I said, *"Andy! Don't call me sir!"* and he said confidently, "I'm sorry SIR—that is our company policy."

Think about your policies—are they for the convenience of your organization, or are they policies that make doing business with you better or quicker?

> *You never need my permission to say yes to a customer. You always need my permission to say no.*
>
> Mitch Lazeran – Owner Bonanza Restaurant

I had some employees from an insurance agency in one of my workshops. They told me their agency decided it didn't want customers "walking in" to pay their bills. So they passed a policy stating customers could mail in payment with no service fee, but they had to pay a $10 service fee if they physically brought it into the office. What do you think the customer response was to this policy? Eventually the insurance agency eliminated it, since it was costing them good customers who were canceling their policies.

Restaurants do the same thing all the time with their "no substitution" policies. You can probably think of examples from credit card companies, airlines, government offices... and the list goes on and on.

ONE SOLUTION—RED & GREEN POLICIES

Differentiating policies is a very valuable tool for all companies and organizations. Policies can generally be divided into two types: red ones and green ones. A red policy is something cast in stone and strictly enforced; non-negotiable. It cannot be changed under any circumstance. It may be a state or federal law, or it may be necessary for customer safety or security. The key with red policies is to explain why they exist and how they benefit the customer. For example, if your company is a wholesaler with a restocking fee for merchandise returns, you might tell a customer, "There is a 10% restocking charge for those returns." Or you might say, "to keep our prices as low as possible and to be fair to all of our customers, we have a 10% restocking charge for return merchandise." Do you see (or hear) the difference?

On the other hand, most policies are *green* policies. These policies are guidelines. Use them when they make sense, but change them when they don't.

> *Make a customer, not a sale.*
>
> Philip Kotler (1931 -   ) PhD and management guru

A story in many customer service books tells of the Seattle bank where a regular customer hands a teller a parking machine card to get it validated. It will save him 75 cents by parking in the bank parking lot. The teller informs him he has to have a transaction, or she can't validate the card. The man explains he's a regular customer, and he was only in the lot for ten minutes while he did some business across the street. The teller will not validate his card, so he asks to speak to the branch manager. She comes over and he explains the story. The manager also refuses to validate the customer's card, saying again it is bank policy. The customer (who owns both a real estate firm and a construction company) promptly closes out his personal and business accounts and transfers them to the bank right across the street, to the tune of more than $1,000,000. THEN he gets his card validated for the transaction!

Look at your return policies, inventory policies, check policies, late fees, service charges and customer service policies. Do they make customer service better, or do they get in the way? I once read a quote that went something like: "It's not the lions and tigers that chase customers away—it's the flies and the gnats." It's the little irritations that cause us to lose a lot of good will and customers!

Someone once asked, "Do you do things by the book or by the brain?" It simply means, think about your responses in customer service situations. You can't have a policy manual covering every possible situation, or it would be ten feet thick. Practice doing what is right rather than hiding behind policies that aren't appropriate in all situations. Doing it "right" for the customer always makes sense.

We are judged on our performance, not our obedience to orders.

Nordstrom employee

ETDBW

I read this acronym somewhere and liked it. It stands for, are you Easy To Do Business With? Think about your policies and procedures. Do you make it easy for people to reach you on the phone, or do you force customers to try to work out their problems with an automated system? Are your hours convenient for your customers or just for your employees?

We had an office supply store in my hometown that closed every day at lunch hour. It was a downtown business and I, also working at a downtown business, could get away at lunch, but could not buy office supplies. They are no longer in business.

Many downtown businesses cling to the 10 – 5 business hours and then complain about Wal-Mart up the road. They haven't adapted to the new customer shopping habits, where up to 70% of the customer's dollar is spent when their store isn't even open! Instead of changing they complain loudly, eventually going out of business, blaming everyone and everything else along the way.

Do you make paperwork so cumbersome for your customers that it irritates them? Do you request information from them that they have already given you? Colonel Sanders from Kentucky Fried Chicken fame used to spout his policy of KISS—or Keep It Simple, Stupid. One author challenges each organization to "Kill a Stupid Rule" and to look for and eliminate the things that irritate or frustrate customers (and employees!).

One of my best friends is a partner in a certified public accounting firm. He is known, and in fact signs some papers,

> *All the rules in the world don't bring out the best in people.*
>
> Larry Harmon – Demar Plumbing

as BTSB. This stands for Buck The System Bob. He is proud of this stature. He refuses to do things that are "standard," because he says not everything or everyone fits neatly in the "box." Instead, he reacts to each customer according to what works best for them, not what works best for the company. Yet, what works best for the customer ultimately DOES work best for the company—especially in the long run!

EMPOWERING EMPLOYEES

World-class companies have found that the more authority they give to the front-line employee, the higher the level of customer satisfaction.

One of the most successful restaurants in my hometown for many years is a chain restaurant called Bonanza. It has been owned and run for almost thirty years by the same owner operators, Mitch and Ed—true examples of customer service Eagles! They have a policy that says, "You never need my permission to say yes to a customer; you always need my permission to say no." They empower employees to do whatever it takes to keep a customer happy or satisfy a request. But, if the employee can't say yes, then Mitch and Ed want to help find a way! They say it's every employee's job to find a way to say "yes" to satisfy guests.

Customers don't like to complain, and normally won't make a big deal about anything. They just want their situation addressed quickly and fairly. It irritates customers (and employees) when the customer service person has to run around trying to find the manager on duty to adjust a customer's bill by a dollar. Give enough authority to the person who is face-to-face with the customer to address routine problems. TRUST them to do a good job.

> *We are there to say yes to people.*
>
> John Dey

Nordstrom's is always mentioned as one of the best retailers when it comes to customer service. They have grown from a single shoe store in Seattle to a multi-billion-dollar company with the idea of empowerment. Here is a card they gave to new employees:

Welcome to Nordstrom.

We are glad to have you with our company.
Our number-one goal is to provide outstanding customer service.
Set both your personal and professional goals high.
We have great confidence in your ability to achieve them.
Nordstrom rules: Rule # 1
Use your good judgment in all situations.

There will be no additional rules. Please feel free to ask your department manager, store manager, or division general manager any questions at any time.

This tells employees they are valuable and trusted. Policies like this increase customer **and employee** satisfaction. Nordstrom also says that as an employee, you will not be criticized for doing too much for a customer, only too little! AND if you are in doubt as to how to proceed, always err in the customer's favor—not in the company's favor. So if you make a mistake, the worst that can happen is sending a customer away *too happy!*

Another favorite eating place for me that exemplifies this point is Outback Steakhouse. Their national advertising slogan is a simple four words: "NO RULES—JUST RIGHT."

Team spirit is what gives so many companies
an edge over their competitors.

George Clements (1932 -) Catholic Priest

With these four words they tell employees and customers, over and over again, that they are there to satisfy and exceed customer expectations, and they regularly do just that. Outback Steakhouse is usually rated one of the best restaurants in the country for customer service and satisfaction.

NON-MANAGEMENT POSITIONS

Employees regularly tell me that management won't let them provide great service; that company policies or procedures get in the way. What can an employee with no authority do?

As a manager and business owner, I loved it when employees came up to me with ideas on how we could improve. I'm not talking about whining here, but an honest desire to improve customer service. I argue that most of the best ideas come from the front-line employee and not the management team. Managers don't spend enough time on the floor or face-to-face with the customers to *really* know what's going on. They don't realize how much simple little changes irritate customers. They don't put up with the comment or criticisms the employee faces regularly because of changes or "great ideas." I BEG you to communicate policies or procedures that upset (and lose) customers to management. You can do this in a positive, constructive way and not be perceived as a whiner or complainer. If management doesn't want to hear your suggestions for improving customer service, then you're probably an Eagle swimming in a duck pond, and you need to find a new home!

> *Nothing should get in the way of providing superior customer service – not even management.*
>
> Jan Carlzon (1941 -) President of Scandinavian Airlines

EAGLE EYE VIEW

- EAGLES examine all policies and procedures regularly.
- EAGLES ask employees (and customers) which policies they have trouble with, and more importantly, what can be done to improve.
- It's the little things that irritate our customers. When it's a small thing, EAGLES usually give in to the customer's wish.
- EAGLES know which policies are red and which are green.
- Establish an authority level allowing the front-line employee to resolve routine problems or complaints.

100% of the shots you don't take, don't go in.

Wayne Gretzky (1961 -) Ice hockey player, coach

I have a new philosophy. I'm only going to dread one day at a time.

Charlie Brown (1950 -) Peanuts character

EXERCISE 10:1

Have an employee or department meeting. Discuss what policies or procedures customers have difficulty with and which they find irritating. Discuss options for what can be done to make it better for the customer. Be sure to identify the "little things" that can cost an organization big money in lost customers. Pick at least one irritating policy you can eliminate or change.

EXERCISE 10:2

For one full week, record every negative customer interaction or problem on a sheet of paper. Include anything that happened when you were not able to totally satisfy a customer, such as an out of stock item, something we don't carry, or a return we would not accept. After the week is up, go over the list with your entire team to see what needs to change or be addressed to reduce the number of "irritants."

EXERCISE 10:3

Make a list of your policies and identify each as either red or green. After each policy on the list, explain the benefit and the reason for each. This helps you understand why they exist, and also helps everyone explain them to the customer.

EXERCISE 10:4

In what ways can your organization "empower" employees more? What are some of the small things needing management approval which really shouldn't need their ok? Establish a level of authority for each person that gives them the opportunity to resolve problems, use their creativity and grow in responsibility.

Exercise daily, eat wisely, die anyway.

Unknown

"Who picked 'I Can't Get No Satisfaction' to be our on-hold music?"

> *Knowing what customers expect is the first and possibly most critical step in delivering quality service.*
>
> Len Berry, PhD Researcher Texas A & M University

11

Exceeding Expectations

A restaurant recently opened in my hometown by the name of "Lagniappe" (pronounced lan-yap). I asked the owner what the name meant, and he said it was "giving a little extra or more than expected." What a great name for a business!

Dr. Leonard Berry, a researcher at Texas A&M University, says we can't just count on "satisfied" customers today. His research shows satisfied customers aren't necessarily loyal customers. If you want loyal customers they need to be *completely* satisfied. This isn't merely a difference in semantics—it's a very real perception held by customers. Put another way, "okay" is no longer okay. Today, customers want more!

The good news is you don't have to wow them every time—just once in a while. For instance, my thirty-year association and loyalty to my insurance agency is based on just a few WOW experiences. I had a fire in one of my restaurants forcing us to close for three months while we remodeled. The insurance company took a position on my loss of income that was very unfavorable to me. When I talked to Bill Hetrick, my agent, he went to bat for me and fought to get a better settlement. He was successful and turned

> *Every guest is a VIP.*
>
> Walt Disney (1901 – 1966) Founder of Walt Disney Company

the "problem" into an opportunity to shine. (Note: Bill is gradually retiring now and my new agent (with the same firm) is Angel – and she is definitely an Eagle as well! Her customer service is outstanding, and I am sure I will be with this agency until I "gradually retire!"

It's impossible to WOW customers every single time we see them. We have way too many customers and not nearly enough time. Plus, if we do try to WOW them each time, their expectations just continue to get higher and higher, and eventually it becomes impossible to WOW them.

Disney doesn't measure guest satisfaction. If they did, it would always be close to 100%. They measure "very satisfied," and from the feedback they receive, they learn and grow by constantly improving on the results.

I think business people instinctively know that in order to get and keep a healthy customer base, they need to exceed expectations. But many—most—don't know how to go about it. You have only to look at advertising to see what I'm talking about.

Why do some businesses use tag lines in their advertising like: *More bang for your buck,* or *More for your money?* The answer: the word "more." They promise more than you'll get anywhere else. Or at least that's what they want you to believe.

More for your money is one way to exceed expectations, but giving more product for the money increases costs. It costs you today, and it costs you tomorrow. The best example of this comes from the auto industry.

I have a friend who was an import car dealer at the time GM came out with its revolutionary 0% financing. She drove past a GM dealer during that month of selling frenzy and worried out loud, "How are we going to compete with

> *Under-promise and over-deliver.*
>
> Tom Peters (1942 -) Writer, management consultant

THAT?" From the back seat, her six-year-old son responded, "But what are they going to do *next* month to sell cars?"

History has answered his question. Every month car manufacturers and dealers announce bigger and bigger rebates, lower interest, zero interest, longer finance terms, free this and free that! I'm waiting for the day they *pay me* to take a new vehicle. People, *we can't buy our customers' loyalty.* The Beatles had it right—"Money can't buy me love..."

What *can* we do? Focus on service. Giving more and more product for less and less money comes from a "take the money and run" business perspective. Giving more service than expected says we're here to stay, in it for the long haul—that we're interested in you, in the community and in the big picture.

While giving more product for the money—more bang for the buck—costs money, giving more service for the money costs next to nothing. You and your co-workers are already there, getting paid. Giving more product for the money makes you vulnerable to the next guy willing to sell the same product for an even tinier profit (or loss). This strategy does not engender loyalty in customers. In fact, quite the opposite is true, it encourages him to constantly shop for the best deal. So why put yourself in that trick bag? The best strategy is to give more service for every dollar. That's the one commodity separating you from all others. They can buy the iPod, the toaster, the insurance policy, the widget from any number of retailers or sources, but they can only get *your* service from YOU.

I purchased a three-hole paper punch claiming to punch forty sheets at one time. Impressive. Or at least it would have been. I couldn't get more than twenty-five sheets in without getting stuck. Petty? Not when you've got reams of

> *Perfection is our goal, excellence will be tolerated.*
>
> J. Yahl (1924 -) British author

paper to punch. They over-promised and under-delivered, and I will not buy another product from that company.

I bought an INFOCUS projector, which I use in my presentations. They advertise their bulb (which costs around $340) has an "average" life of 2,000 hours. I've gone through seven bulbs now, and not one of them has even 500 hours on it before burning out. In fact, only one made it past 400. The company's lackluster response to my calls and e-mails? "They are only guaranteed for ninety days." They are unwilling (read: uncaring) to do *anything* for me. So I tell this story over and over to the thousands of attendees at my seminars and will not purchase from them again. Customers not only vote with their feet, they take others with them!

Customer expectations come from many places: previous experience with you, from your competition, and from what you tell them to expect in your advertising. I once passed a McDonald's restaurant with a sign proclaiming: "We have the world's friendliest employees!" What are patrons expecting when they go in? Don't set yourself up to fail in customer expectations by making promises you can't keep. If you advertise you give fast service, don't be upset when your customers want quick service.

UNDER-PROMISE AND OVER-DELIVER

I purchased 500 pens from Amsterdam Printing. I give the pens as a "thank you" to clients. They cost approximately $2 each. When I ordered them, they were advertised as "four assorted colors," but when they arrived, there were only three colors—with the color I liked most, missing. I called Amsterdam Printing to tell them I was not happy. They immediately apologized, said someone should have called to tell me they were out of the fourth color and then offered

> *There are no traffic jams when you go the extra mile.*
>
> Roger Staubach (1942 -   ) NFL star quarterback

to send me 125 pens in the missing color. I said, "That'll be great. How do you want me to return the other 125 pens?" They told me to keep them as their apology. THAT exceeded my expectations!

But the story doesn't end there. A year later, I noticed the ink had dried in some of the pens still on hand. I called Amsterdam to complain. They apologized once more and explained that the ink would dry over time, but they would be happy to send replacement refills for all the pens I had at no charge. THAT AGAIN exceeded my expectations!

In the ten years I have done business with Amsterdam Printing, I have had two problems. They resolved both in ways that exceeded my expectations. As a result, I am a loyal customer who has not only placed numerous orders, I have told these stories to a LOT of people.

What happens when you exceed customer expectations? You build loyalty, for one. But you also set the standard for what your customers expect from you in the future. People like consistency. Look at McDonald's. They may not serve gourmet cuisine, but their customers know the burger they order in Nashville will taste the same as the burger they got in Seattle. Constantly meeting the expectations they set forth for their customers has made McDonald's a very successful global enterprise.

As discussed in preceding chapters, it's a battle to earn the loyalty of our customers. Once earned, don't make the mistake of taking it for granted or thinking you can relax your standards. Winning the battle does not ensure you will win the war!

My wife and I went to a restaurant that had just opened in our community. The salad bar was fantastic, with lots of fresh fruit and crispy vegetables. We loved it, and returned

> *Our strongest competition*
> *is our own reputation.*
> Disney University

the following weekend with another couple. We were disappointed to find the salad bar half as stocked as the week before, with many of our favorite items missing. When I asked the server about it, she shrugged, saying, "Oh, we just had extra stuff out there for our grand opening." That's not a good long-term business strategy. Less than a year later they had even fewer things on their salad bar, right before their "grand closing."

SOQNOP

Remember this: Sell On Quality, Not On Price. If we try to compete with everyone willing to sell products the cheapest, we will find no matter how low we drop our prices, there is always someone out there willing to sell for even less. Even if they sell for a loss, some idiots think they can make it up in volume! It's an ugly scenario. Do you really want to play on that field? Put yourself at that level? Someone once said, "It's like wrestling a pig: You both get dirty, but only the pig enjoys it!" You CAN win by providing exceptional service. Customers WILL reward you for that. You've heard it before: It's the sizzle of the steak that keeps them coming back.

TIMELINESS

In trying to exceed our customers' expectations, one cannot ignore TIME. It's critical to our success. But what is timely to you may not be timely to your customers. Guess who matters most?

Michael Stephenson, a columnist for a Texas newspaper, wrote about a personal experience at a hotel chain that advertised "free continental breakfast." When he went to get

> *We decided to be 1% better at 100 things*
> *instead of being 100% better at one thing.*
> Jan Carlzon (1941 -) President of Scandinavian Airlines

his breakfast, he was told it didn't start until 7:30. As he and many guests were already gone by that time, he complained to the desk clerk, who informed him they get lots of complaints about the 7:30 time. Stephenson asked why, having received so many complaints, did they not change the time? In total seriousness the clerk responded, "That's when the boy delivers the doughnuts."

When I go into McDonald's my concept of timeliness is different than when I go to a fine dining restaurant. Eagles are cognizant of what customers consider "timely," and do everything in their power to meet those expectations of timeliness.

How many times have you gone into a large store where there are dozens of employees, but only one cashier with a line of customers waiting to pay? How wise is it to make customers wait, to make it inconvenient for them to give us money?

Everyone in the organization should be tuned in to how long customers wait to pay or get help. It is a major source of customer dissatisfaction. Many stores regularly find abandoned merchandise by the registers, left by customers who changed their minds in frustration. They wanted the product(s); they just didn't want to be made to suffer the wait.

If you're open 24/7, someone should be watching out for the customer 24/7. My local building supply store, Menard's, has a sign over the checkouts stating, "If there are more than two people in line, we will open another register." Across the street at Target, clerks with no one at their registers wait in the aisle, watching for customers ready to check out. They cheerfully say, "I can help you!"

I am frequently in hotels in my line of work. I can't understand how they can spend millions of dollars on décor,

> *If you make yourself a doormat,*
> *you will get stepped on.*
> American Proverb

yet neglect to staff the front desk properly during premium check-in and check-out times. There are many times during your day that are predictably busier, be prepared for them.

SEGMENTING

Let's not make the mistake of lumping our customers together in one category. They are all unique individuals with different needs and wants. Different expectations. Let's focus on what makes them individuals, what makes each one unique.

Do you know your customers' names? Do you know how much they spend and on what? Do you know what they like? We can't begin to exceed expectations if we don't even know what they expect. Eagles use their database to get to know their customers better. They collect information, conduct surveys and learn what their customers want, need or think about. Take time to visit with them. Go to their place of business. See the challenges they face. Track customer preferences in products and services. Airlines do this very successfully with frequent-flyers and first-class passengers. There are hotels that note if a customer prefers fiber-filled or down pillows. That's the best part: If we just listen to our customers, they will tell us how we can meet their expectations. Only then can we hope to exceed them.

CUSTOMER SERVICE CULTURE

Create a customer service *culture* within your organization. Culture means there is an invisible, but very real, atmosphere within your organization that puts the customer first—decisions are not based solely on the bottom line, but on how they improve the relationship with the customer.

> *Here is a simple but powerful rule – always give people more than what they expect to get.*
>
> Nelson Boswell (1740 – 1795) British writer, journalist

This philosophy becomes a culture when every single person, from the CEO to the guy on the loading dock, feels it. Everyone in the company knows they exist at the whim of the customer. You create a culture that puts priority on enhancing the relationship with the customer by giving employees the authority to make decisions—the authority to act on the customers' behalf. If you create this culture, starting at the top, it will spread to every person within your organization. Instead of micro-managing your people, you mold their behavior by catching them doing something right. You praise them in public, correct missteps in private. If you build this culture, they—good customers and great employees—will come.

One of the best examples of success as a result of exceeding expectations is Fed-Ex, or Federal Express. Fred Smith and his fellow classmates at Yale University were given the assignment to come up with an original business concept. Smith wrote a paper on an overnight delivery service. His professor thought the idea was highly improbable and gave Smith a "C." After all, who could compete with the service and low cost of the U.S. Postal Service? Undeterred, Smith founded Federal Express. By 1997, the company was worth $16 billion, and Smith's personal fortune exceeded $700 million.

Smith achieved this phenomenal success by exceeding the expectations millions of us had regarding the delivery of packages and letters. Conditioned by the U.S. Postal Service, we expected and accepted slower delivery. The Postal Service has been an absolutely amazing delivery system, but in recent decades the only thing it raised were its rates. Service was lagging. After waiting in long lines, customers

> *People perform best and deliver the best customer service when they like what they do.*
>
> Unknown

faced unfriendly and uncaring clerks. Mail got lost or stolen. Jokes abounded about "snail mail."

Enter Fed-Ex with its seemingly impossible guarantee (we all know it—say it with me): "When it absolutely, positively, must get there overnight!" Smith and each and every one of Fed-Ex's employees dedicated themselves to delivering what they promised, and then some. Smith empowered his employees to make decisions consistent with the Fed-Ex guarantee. They did whatever it took. Thanks to Smith's brilliant management style, Fed-Ex stories soon became urban legends.

I recall hearing of the time a blizzard in the Rocky Mountains grounded all commercial aircraft in Colorado. Fed-Ex was transporting an organ for an ailing patient awaiting surgery. A Fed-Ex employee took the initiative to hire a private helicopter—at great expense to the company—in order to deliver the organ on time. Instead of being reprimanded for authorizing such a huge expenditure, the employee was commended for his actions.

SET YOUR STANDARDS

You can't exceed expectations until you know what they are. If you don't even know your standards, how can you expect your customers to figure it out? Unless you define your business model, know what level of quality you intend to deliver in terms of goods and/or services, you are at the fickle mercy of the winds of commerce. You constantly end up reacting instead of acting, chasing instead of leading.

Too often, I have seen these businesses fail. Their owners scratch their heads and wonder, "What happened?" They failed to define themselves and who their customers were.

> *Seldom does an individual exceed*
> *his own expectations.*
>
> Unknown

Define your standards, set your goals, measure your progress, and your chances for success improve dramatically.

CUSTOMER EXPECTATIONS

Most customer service expectations are based on accumulated experiences with other businesses. Because of this—sadly for the customer—the bar is pretty low. But, good news for you! It's an easier target! By just doing a little more than your competition, you will shine.

Customer expectations are also based on what you have led them to believe they can expect from you. Make sure you can deliver, before you make these assertions.

EMPLOYEE EXPECTATIONS

Too often employers overlook their employees' expectations. This is how labor unions and government agencies like OSHA were created. A good employee expects his workplace to be safe and comfortable. She expects to be treated with courtesy and compensated fairly. Employers too focused on a fat bottom line make the mistake of trying to attain it by overlooking or skimping on employee needs. That's always a mistake, because it's our employees who make us money. It is our employees who are on the front line with our customers. By taking good care of our employees, we take good care of our customers. I feel very strongly that happy employees make for happy customers.

A good friend of mine owns a landscape company. In an industry where minimum wage and no benefits is the norm, he pays much higher than the going rate, provides excellent health insurance (for which he pays the entire premium), and surprises his employees with bonuses throughout the

> *People with tact have less to retract.*
>
> Arnold Glasgow

year. He started a retirement fund for them and contributes generously to it. Does he sound crazy or, at least, too altruistic? You decide. His crew has a reputation in the community for being extremely efficient; they meet or beat the project deadline every time. Cost overruns are non-existent. They are highly skilled; no other landscape company in our community even comes close. My friend's crew is extremely loyal; his core group has been with him since he started his company. (How much does it cost us to train new employees?) Because of their skill and loyalty, they need almost no supervision. Once given instructions on the project, they get to work and my friend can line up new projects without worrying about what's occurring at the job site.

Oh—and here's the other thing: His business margins and profits are probably the highest of his industry in the entire area. Though he is the most expensive, he's always booked because he's the best. He started out with that as his standard, and his crew delivers.

Noah's Ark in Wisconsin Dells is one of the biggest water parks in the country. A seasonal business, Noah's Ark relies heavily on college students who are home for the summer, to staff the park. The entire city of Wisconsin Dells depends on the tourist trade, so it's a challenge to get enough quality employees to fill the thousands of summer jobs. But year after year, Noah's Ark gets their pick of the best employees. How do they do this? With excellent employee training and good wages. At the end of the season, Noah's Ark rewards its staff by giving away hundreds of gifts, from DVD players to the grand prize: a new car. The prizes are awarded based on scores employees receive from customers' comment cards. How do you suppose guests to Noah's Ark are treated? Like royalty! Not only does Noah's Ark never worry

> *Failure is the foundation of success.*
>
> Lao Tzu

about staffing, they get an additional reward. With a guest-focused staff, Noah's Ark's safety record is one of the highest in the industry. As safety went up, insurance premiums went down!

ANTICIPATE NEEDS

One of the most effective ways to exceed customer expectations is to anticipate their needs. The best way to do this is to put yourself in their shoes and ask, "What would please me in this situation?"

I am reminded of the British Airways commercial showing a man in his office at the end of the day. He's ready to relax; a glass of champagne and a golf magazine magically appear next to him. Smiling, he picks up the magazine and realizes his glasses need cleaning. A box of tissues appear. He kicks off his shoes and is ready to kick back. The chair becomes a recliner. The message? British Airways anticipates your needs.

Walgreens is terrific at anticipating needs. They automatically refill or remind you when a prescription needs to be refilled. The check-outs are surrounded by items we all need, but often forget to pick up. Besides offering drugs, medicines, and the like, Walgreens has stuff people often run out of, like milk and dog food. They are conveniently located; you don't have to travel far to find one. The clerks are helpful and encourage you to try new products without risk. If you aren't happy with any product, just bring it back for a refund.

If there was nothing wrong in the world there wouldn't be anything for us to do.

George Bernard Shaw (1856 - 1950) Irish playwright

PUT YOURSELF IN YOUR CUSTOMERS' POSITION

Since we ARE customers for most of our lives, it should be easy to put ourselves in our customers' position. It's just a matter of awareness. What would a service person need to do to make you feel special? If you were on the other side of the desk or counter, how would you want to be treated? Treat them the same way. What could someone do to go above and beyond your expectations? What would impress you if you were the customer? EAGLES actions reflect this attitude and they succeed at exceeding!

A LITTLE SOMETHING EXTRA—LSEs

This means remembering customers' names, their birthdays and anniversaries. Recognizing and rewarding employees for doing that little something extra. Dropping customers off at the shopping mall while their car is being serviced, knowing customers' tastes and buying habits and making recommendations accordingly, or recognizing when a client may be eligible for lower insurance premiums.

I know a car dealer in Milwaukee, Wisconsin who, when asked if he rented cars, told the customer, "We have service loaner cars, but no rentals." The disappointed couple had hoped to rent a nice car for their honeymoon. The dealer responded by loaning them his personal car. A year later the couple returned to buy a Lexus.

I know a manager who puts a handful of pennies in his right-hand pocket every morning. Each time he gives a compliment or does a "little something extra," he transfers a penny from the right pocket to the left. During the day the pennies on the right serve as a constant reminder to make others feel good. At the end of the day, if his left pocket is

> *Too much of a good thing can be wonderful!*
>
> Mae West (1893 - 1980) American actress

full and the right side is empty, he sleeps better knowing he's done a good job of making people feel good that day.

When Disney Studio was producing the breakthrough movie *Who Framed Roger Rabbit?*, they combined live-action with animation. Disney wanted to make the union between cartoon and humans seamless and the experience for the viewers extraordinary. Disney wanted each frame to be a WOW! The process was tedious and expensive. There was a scene in which Roger Rabbit is chased around a room. It was a hilarious scene, but when Disney execs first viewed it, they felt it lacked realism. Even though it was animated, they wanted it to be "real." They told the animators to "bump the lamp." Adding hundreds of thousands of dollars to the cost of making the film, animators had Roger bump a lamp hanging over a table and send shadows spinning wildly.

Would the viewers' experience have been diminished if the lamp remained still? Probably not, but with that attitude—one of providing viewers with the ultimate experience—Disney had a huge hit on its hands. Look for your ways to "bump the lamp".

PAY IT FORWARD

Two movies, *Crash* and *Pay it Forward*, focused attention on the fact that our lives are all interconnected, and the disastrous, rippling effects a cruel act of indifference can have. But, just as a person who was treated rudely may take it out on the next guy, an act of kindness can have the opposite result. Exceed someone's expectations and that person leaves with head high, smiling broadly. How do you suppose he treats the people he encounters the rest of the day? You—YOU—can change the world with one kind, thoughtful act!

HAVE FUN WITH YOUR CUSTOMERS AND CO-WORKERS

There is so much doom and gloom in the world. Just turn on the news and you're bombarded with it. Most people don't want to feel bad; they want to feel good. Humor goes a long way toward helping this happen. We can help by keeping things light. Our customers and employees will appreciate it.

When Fox News celebrated its tenth anniversary, Greta Van Susteren, host of the popular show "On The Record", said she had more fun in her first week at Fox than in the previous three years at her former network. The attitude that pervades Fox News has enabled it to take on and compete with network giants.

Humor is a very powerful drug that creates fond and lasting memories for our customers and co-workers. We can take our *work* seriously without taking *ourselves* seriously. While humor can help humanize us and bring us close to our customers, there are times when humor is inappropriate. It should never be used at someone else's expense. And not everyone will appreciate it or "get" it.

Southwest Airlines understands and accepts that out of one hundred people there is one who will not appreciate the humor. Southwest CEO Herb Kelleher once got a letter from a disgruntled customer complaining that the joking around lacked professionalism. She thought flying was serious business and everyone should take it that way. She warned she would not fly Southwest Airlines in the future unless they changed their ways. Herb wrote back saying, "We will miss you." He believes if 99% like what you're doing, you don't put it at risk for the sake of pleasing one person.

MEASURE YOUR PROGRESS

As discussed in Chapter 3, you may think you're doing a good job, but unless you measure it, do you really know? Just as important as measuring your business health with a monthly financial statement, you want to track the health of your customer relationships. Once you establish a baseline, you can measure and monitor your progress toward not only satisfying customers' needs, but in exceeding their expectations.

EAGLE EYE VIEW

- EAGLES under-promise and over-deliver.
- EAGLES SOQNOP: Sell On Quality, Not On Price.
- EAGLES create a customer service CULTURE.
- EAGLES set and maintain standards.
- EAGLES know what customers expect from them.
- EAGLES anticipate needs.
- EAGLES do a "Little Something Extra."
- EAGLES have fun.
- EAGLES measure progress.

Life is either a daring adventure or nothing.

Helen Keller (1880 – 1968) Deafblind author, activist

EXERCISE 11:1

For one week, keep track of every interaction you have with either an internal or external customer. Note how many times you were able to do a little something extra to exceed his or her expectations. Work at increasing the number of times you're successful at it.

EXERCISE 11:2

Meet with co-workers and make up two lists. The first one is the top-five things you can do every time you interact with a co-worker. The second list is the top-five things you can do when you interact with an external customer to exceed her expectations. Then start doing those things as frequently as you can during the week.

EXERCISE 11:3

Time is important to customers. Look at the process a customer goes through when dealing with your organization. Do you respect his time at every point? Can anything be done to provide service in a quicker or simplified way? What steps can you eliminate or speed up?

EXERCISE 11:4

Employees who are able to have fun are more likely to enjoy and have fun with customers. What can you do as an organization to have more fun each day? What specific activities could you develop or encourage?

The great thing in this life is not so much where we are, but in what direction we are moving.

Oliver Wendell Holmes (1809 – 1894) Physician, writer

Nothing great has ever been achieved without enthusiasm.

Ralph Waldo Emerson (1803 – 1882) Essayist, poet

My decision is maybe – and that's final!

Sign on a managers desk

"If you're not completely satisfied, your money will be cheerfully refunded as soon as we can find someone around here who's cheerful."

If I died,
would that
make you happy?

Customer service person to unhappy customer

12

Problems and Complaints

There's an old joke that the definition of a bank is a place that loans you an umbrella when the sun is shining, then asks for it back when it starts to rain. My banker, Don St. Germaine from *Baybank,* has a loyal customer for life because that doesn't describe him or his bank.

I can't tell you in just 200-plus pages about all the problems and troubles I have had in business. At my lowest point, Don was there to help—and I'm not just talking about lending me more money to get into more trouble. I'm talking about listening, helping, and counseling me to make good financial decisions. Eagles know when they can help customers with problems. They create a loyalty that cannot be "bought" with a loan rate that is a half percentage point less.

Now, what about customers who have a problem with us or our business? If you have read and applied the lessons in the previous eleven chapters, you can skip this one and go right on to the last chapter.

Just kidding! Sort of. Because the best scenario regarding problems and complaints is not to have many. Prevention is far better than requiring a cure. Seriously taking to heart everything we have discussed thus far and putting the principles into action will prevent innumerable problems and

> *Your customers will get better when you do.*
>
> Unknown

their ugly step-sisters -- complaints -- from darkening your door regularly.

But here in the real world, "shift happens," as Southwest Airlines says. We will have problems. People will complain. So, let's deal with it.

Dan opened a small independent restaurant called Border Grill in my hometown several years ago. My wife and I became instant regulars as we loved the food but more importantly the service he and his staff provided. Here was a "flock of eagles"! An early incident told us much more about Dan and his Eagle behavior. We arrived at home with our take-out order and sat down to eat. Unfortunately, the burritos had both cheese and sour cream on them which we always request be left off. We were both hungry and disappointed. I called the restaurant and talked to an EAGLE who told me they would make up another order and deliver it to our home immediately. Nice recovery! About 15 minutes later, Dan, the owner, was at our door with our new order, an apology and a little extra treat! He turned it from a negative to a positive experience that ten years later we still remember!

So, let's start by looking at our attitude. Most of the time a complaining customer triggers our "fight or flight" mode, does it not? Most of us are uncomfortable, fearful, apprehensive, anxious, angry, or feel other negative emotions. That's good if, wanting to avoid those negative emotions in the future, it motivates us to prevent future occurrences.

So, let's learn to look at problems and complaints as an opportunity. Instead of fearing them, how about embracing them as a means to learn? To improve. To find the flaws in the system so we can correct them. An opportunity to better

> *Right or wrong, the customer is always right.*
>
> Marshall Field (1834 – 1906) Founder of Marshall Fields

train our staff and enhance our delivery of goods and/or services to our customers. Best of all, problems and complaints are a great way to turn a disgruntled, unhappy customer into a friend and customer for life.

Find that hard to believe? It is my experience that some of my best, i.e. most loyal, customers started off complaining. Think about it: a complaining customer is emotional. In previous chapters we spent a good deal of time discussing how to create positive emotions and tap into the well of customer emotions. Emotions are extremely powerful. The most effective advertisers know this well.

When we are able to take a customer experiencing negative emotions, such as anger and frustration, and turn those into positive emotions, we win a huge victory.

Effectively handling problems and complaints gives us and our organization a unique opportunity to shine. Customers understand that, because we are fallible human beings, mistakes occur. Based on past experiences with other companies, they expect us to meet their complaint with complacency or an uncaring attitude. Based on past experiences, they don't think their problem will be solved or their questions answered. They don't even expect an apology. Sad, isn't it?

BUT, THEY WANT ONE!

Follow the steps I am about to lay out, and you will turn more upset customers into loyal patrons. You will become one of the most valuable employees in your company. You will become so adept and successful at handling complaints that, instead of dreading them, you will welcome them. I say this unequivocally and without the slightest exaggeration.

> *A customer who complains is my best friend.*
>
> - Stew Leonard owner of Stew Leonard's Supermarkets

What follows makes the tool you hold in your hand, this book, worth a hundred times the selling price.

LISTEN

As helpless infants, we absorb our environment through our ears. We quickly learn to recognize the voices of our mother and father—our survival depends on them! We learn a very complicated language through listening. As human beings, listening is one of the first things we learn and may be the most important.

Listen *completely* to what your customer is saying. Let him blow off steam if he is angry. Listen to *fully understand why* your customer is upset. Be respectful and compassionate.

Look at your customer. Don't let your eyes or thoughts wander. This person feeds you and your family, pays your rent or mortgage and car payment. He'll send your kids to college and buy flowers for your mom. You owe him your full, undivided attention.

Listen with an open mind. It is typical human behavior to become defensive when confronted. Unfortunately, when we are in a defensive position, we are also closed minded and less likely to find common ground and a solution.

If the customer is loud, aggressive, or disruptive to other customers, move to a private area, preferably one with seating. Invite him to sit; he will be less aggressive than if he remains standing.

Let him vent. Get it all out. He'll feel much better after he gets rid of all that venom. And only once he's fully vented can he even listen to anything you say. If you want him to listen to you, you must listen to him first.

> *Admit your errors before someone else exaggerates them.*
>
> Dr. Andrew V. Mason, Surgeon

DO NOT INTERRUPT!

Don't just listen for an opportunity to jump in with your arguments, "But..." "Well..."

Listen for understanding. Look past the anger and frustration to the human being with a problem who has come to you for help. Listen to fully understand what is bothering him. Sometimes customers complain about one thing, but it's really about something else. Some other emotion might be coming into play. (The car wasn't fixed right, she almost had an accident, her kids were in the car...) Listen for a solution. Only when we truly understand the problem we are facing can we come up with the right strategy to resolve it. A quarterback facing fourth down and 10 on his own twenty yard line will probably call a different play than he would on a first and goal on the three. You must adjust for the specific situation.

DON'T TAKE IT PERSONALLY

Although you might be on the receiving end of the customer's wrath, it usually isn't you, personally, with whom she is angry or upset. She is upset over the situation, the problem. You just happen to be in a unique position: you can do something about it. That is, as long as you leave your own emotions out of it. Research found more than 50% of all complaints are presented to front-line people. If that is you, it is because your company has faith and confidence in your ability to take excellent care of its valuable customers.

Granted, no one likes being yelled at, it is extremely uncomfortable. But if you keep your emotions out of it and just focus on the problem, you allow yourself to be on the customer's side. Focus on the problem and not on their be-

> *Don't find fault,*
> *find a remedy.*
>
> Henry Ford (1863 – 1947) Founder of Ford Motor Company

havior. Think about offering them great service even if they may not deserve it! You can see things from his/her perspective. From this vantage point you are a more effective intermediary, a problem solver. The customer will feel this and be far more receptive to finding an amicable solution. Always remain calm and in control.

EMPATHIZE

Once the customer has fully vented, show him you understand by expressing empathy for his situation. You must be sincere. If you have listened seeking understanding, you are able to put yourself in his shoes and feel his frustration. Let him know this by saying things like, "I understand your frustration. If this happened to me I would be mad, too." Make sure you acknowledge their feelings.

APOLOGIZE

Immediately apologize to your customer. He has taken the time and courtesy (yes, courtesy, he is giving you an opportunity to fix the problem and to keep him as a customer!) to bring this to your attention. At the very least he deserves a sincere apology. Again, the key word is sincere. Don't offer some lame, fake apology which comes off like a flat "Have a nice day..." Make it heartfelt. Remember, this person helps feed you and your family!

Be careful with your apologies and your exact wording. Saying, "I am sorry we did that to you," may cost you a lot of money in a lawsuit where lawyers will try to prove you admitted you wronged the customer. Alternatively, you can always say, "I am sorry for the inconvenience," or "I am sorry

> *Customer complaints are the*
> *schoolbooks from which we learn.*
>
> Unknown

you feel that way," which apologizes for the situation without admitting blame (unless you WANT to admit blame).

OWN IT

Own the complaint and deal with it immediately. Do not say things like "I can't help you with that..." "This isn't my department..." "...not my job..." "You'll have to talk to a manager..." No, this person is talking to **YOU**, right now! Better to deal with it and move on. If you are truly not authorized to deal with complaints get the customer face to face with someone who is by saying something relevant to the situation like, "How aggravating your order was lost—I am so sorry that happened. I am going to page my supervisor; she will resolve this for you." Stay with the situation until it is resolved—never leave a customer in limbo. Take responsibility and take action!

RESOLVE THE PROBLEM

Many times the solution is easy and obvious. An exchange of defective merchandise, replacement of an item, an adjustment on a bill, or no charge for a bad meal.

Other problems are more complex. In those situations you need to clarify the problem. So both you and your customer know you understand the full nature of the complaint, repeat it back to him/her. "If I understand you correctly, you are upset because_______. Is that right?"

Ask how he/she would like you to resolve the situation. Many times, the request is reasonable and within your ability to grant. Sometimes all she wants is an apology. Other times she asks for the moon and the stars. Don't tell her

> *Blessed are the flexible – for they shall not be bent out of shape.*
>
> Michael McGriff - Poet

what you *can't* or *won't* do, tell her what you *can* or are *willing* to do. "Here's what I can do..." "I'd be happy to..." Ask if that will satisfy her. "Will that resolve it to your satisfaction?" "Will you be happy with that?" "Would that take care of it for you?"

I was staying at a hotel and an alarm went off at 4:30 a.m. in the next room. It was a loud, obnoxious buzzer. I assumed there was no one in the room as it continued to buzz and kept me awake for over an hour. At 6 a.m., my alarm joined in to make it a duet.

When I checked out, the clerk asked if everything was okay. I told her about the annoying alarm clock (which was still buzzing). Her response was a very dissatisfying, "Yeah, that happens." Why did she ask if she wasn't prepared to help do something, or at least apologize?

Now, what was I looking for? I didn't want a free room or discount; I just wanted to be heard. I wanted a little empathy, understanding, and an apology. I wanted her to say she would remind housekeeping to switch off alarms so future guests would not be inconvenienced. That's all. It could have been so easy, and would have made a difference in how I feel about that hotel.

Finally, when it comes to resolving a problem, do it quickly. The longer you let a problem exist, the more customers tend to exaggerate it, and the more people they tell about it. Solve it as quickly as you possibly can.

ELEVATE IT

Sometimes, no matter what we do, we can not satisfy a customer. Sometimes a personality issue or other aspect

> *Customers don't expect us to be perfect. They do expect you to fix things when they go wrong.*
>
> Donald Porter – V. P. British Airways

gets in the way of resolving the problem and keeping the customer. Maybe the customer has pushed all your buttons and you are about to unload on them. When this happens, it is time to take the issue to the next level. Your manager or supervisor typically has more experience in these cases, and she may look at something differently and see a solution. She may have more authority to offer something you are not authorized to offer.

Another interesting thing that happens frequently (and that I'm sure you have seen before) is that irate customer will be nicer to your boss or supervisor than they were to you! This can be frustrating, but it does happen regularly when resolving complaints. The customer has vented on you, gotten it out of his system, and now he is ready to work on a solution. Don't take it personally. You have served a necessary function in the process.

THANK THE CUSTOMER

Thank him for bringing the issue to your attention, for giving you the opportunity to correct the situation and retain him as a customer. He really is doing you a huge favor. Most people hate confrontation, and would rather take their business elsewhere than become irate with you. One day you'd realize you hadn't seen so-and-so for quite some time, and you would never know he gave his business to someone else. If enough customers follow suit, you'd soon be another dried up duck pond!

Government research statistics show that twenty-four out of twenty-five customers—a whopping 96%—won't complain to you. But they will complain to someone else about you! Be complaint-friendly. Ask for feedback. If you are

> *Be soft on people but tough on the problem.*
>
> Unknown

proactive, if people feel like their issues will be resolved, you have an increased opportunity to turn these people into loyal customers.

So, thank him sincerely: "Mr. Jones, I am so sorry this happened, and thank you so much for letting me know so I could take care of it. We appreciate your feedback." You could take it further by offering your personal assistance in the future: "Here is my card with my personal extension (e-mail, cell number). If you have any questions or concerns in the future, please contact me directly."

ONE STEP FURTHER

Once a complaint is solved, our tendency is to move on quickly, dropping it like we've just grabbed a hot skillet. But, now that you've solved the problem, take it one step further and ask, "What else may I help you with?"

One step further can mean doing something extra to make it up to the customer. Depending on your company policies, this can be anything from a coupon for a free car wash, a discount toward his next purchase, or a complimentary dinner. The customer will not be expecting this, and it will more than likely leave them feeling positive about you.

No matter what, we need to make sure our customer leaves feeling better than she did before complaining. We need to heal her feelings. Feelings are everything, remember? To borrow ServePro's motto, "Like it never even happened." We can't erase what happened, but we can do everything in our power to help the customer feel better for having talked to

> *Nothing gives one person so much advantage over another as to remain always cool and unruffled under all circumstance.*
>
> Thomas Jefferson (1743 – 1826) 3rd U.S. President

us about it. Most of that is accomplished through listening, empathizing, apologizing, resolving, and thanking.

LEARN FROM IT

If we didn't learn from our mistakes, we'd still be crawling instead of walking. If the same complaint keeps coming up, please do something to resolve it permanently. In staff meetings, talk about the types of complaints you get and brainstorm for solutions. Your company will be healthier for it. "Fail forward" means when we make mistakes we learn from them.

BE PROACTIVE

In his book, *The Seven Habits of Highly Successful People*, Stephen Covey lists the number-one habit as "Being Proactive." This means the ability to see things and take care of things. It can be anything from picking up a piece of trash by your front door to complex problem-solving. Proactive people look for ways to improve things. They are on top of it. People who are proactive get raises, have more job security, and get promoted more frequently. A proactive person gets things done and becomes invaluable to his employer.

Proactive is preventive. You've heard "The best defense is a good offense." A proactive person prevents problems and complaints by being alert. He straightens the rug before someone trips on it, makes sure systems run efficiently. He is constantly on the look out for ways to improve. We already know this at our deepest core. It is age-old wisdom

> *When you begin your journey to resolve a conflict, always take your first few steps in their shoes.*
>
> Joe Constance (1955 -) Entrepreneur

our elders tried to instill in us with aphorisms like:

> *An ounce of prevention is worth a pound of cure.*
> *A stitch in time saves nine.*
> *Nip it in the bud.*
> *The early bird gets the worm.*
> *The early worm gets eaten. (Just kidding!)*

A proactive person can tell if a customer isn't completely happy. She has a sixth sense about it. Most customers won't tell you they aren't happy, but their body language tells you otherwise.

Another way to be proactive is to "invite" complaints by being complaint-friendly. If our customers are unhappy, we need to be accessible to them. Some companies have 800 numbers and dedicated phone lines staffed by live service reps just for this purpose. Talk about letting customers know they are important!

You can have comment cards available for your customers. Comments tell us what we are doing right. More importantly, where we are failing our customers' expectations. Customers feel uncomfortable with confrontation, causing a scene, or making *you* feel bad by complaining. While they might not complain to your face, they *will* talk about it with their friends and family. Providing them with a comment card to vent eases some of the negative feelings and gives you a chance to correct the situation. Allow the customer to remain anonymous, if he prefers.

The internet gives our customers unprecedented access to us. Your website should invite customers to "contact us," with instructions for e-mailing or phoning. The easier we

> *I am at a time in my life where I realize I don't have to get angry with someone who disagrees with me.*
>
> Bill Clinton (1946 -) 42nd U.S. President

make it to resolve issues between us, the better our relationships with our customers will be.

To help staff remember the steps in handling a customer complaint, Baptist Hospitals in Florida & Alabama use the acronym **ACT**, which stands for "Apologize, Correct+, and Trend." "Correct Plus" means to fix it and then do something to make up for the inconvenience the customer suffered. "Trend" means to fix it and then make sure you learn from it.

I like this acronym from the book *Up Your Service* by Ron Kaufman: **SERVICE**.

S – Say you're sorry

E – Expedite solution

R – Respond

V – Victory to the customer

I – Implement improvements

C – Communicate results

E – Extend the outcome

Another one I received from Dan Nelson at the Hampton Inn in Rochester, Minnesota is, "Take the **HEAT**!"

H – Hear it

E – Empathize

A – Act on it and solve it

T – Thank them

Use whatever works to get the service results you want and need.

> *It's not that I am so smart, it's just that I stay with the problems longer.*
>
> Albert Einstein (1879 – 1955) Theoretical physicist

If you can't seem to connect or resolve a customer's problem or complaint, try this advice: "Don't retreat; advance in another direction." Look at the problem from another angle, ask someone else for help or advice, get help from books like this one, or ask for a "time-out." Sometimes the light of a new day brings the right solution. If a solution doesn't immediately present itself, ask the customer to give you some time to resolve it. Tell him you will get in touch with him at a specified time and will have an answer for him then. You will be amazed at how cooperative customers can be when they know you are working on their behalf.

A small number of customers complain for the sole purpose of taking advantage of us. Fortunately those customers are a small minority, about 1 to 2%. The problem comes when you try to catch those few. Sometimes you will guess wrong and offend an honestly unhappy good customer. Nordstrom says those few people are just a cost of doing business. Accept it.

If acronyms help you remember the steps necessary to resolve customer complaints, here's one more: The Disney organization has used the acronym **LAST.**

L – Listen
A – Apologize
S – Solve the problem
T – Thank the customer

Remember the "LAST" acronym when handling customer problems and complaints, and you will build *LASTing* relationships!

Fall seven times, stand up eight.

Japanese Proverb

IS THE CUSTOMER ALWAYS RIGHT?

This is the tough question many companies still strongly profess to be true. Having owned and operated nine different businesses, I can unequivocally answer this question with a resounding NO! Everyone who has worked in customer service knows some customers lie, some make mistakes, some steal, and some cheat. World-class companies say it a little differently. They say, "The customer is not always right—but they are always the customer." What does that mean? It simply says to try and resolve the problem, no matter who is right. Try to save a customer and save a relationship.

EAGLE EYE VIEW

- Problems and complaints are a reality of doing business.
- Having an effective strategy to successfully deal with problems and complaints lessens their sting and leads to better relationships with your customers.
- Successful resolution of problems and complaints replaces fear with confidence. EAGLES come to embrace complaints as a means of strengthening business and improving service to customers.
- EAGLES known to be effective at solving problems and complaints become VERY VALUABLE employees!
- The steps necessary to successfully resolve problems and complaints are:

  Listen. Do not interrupt, do not take it personally.

  Empathize. Feel what it must have been like for this person. Put yourself in his shoes.

  Apologize. Be sincere! Often, this is all our customers want: to be heard, understood, and offered a sincere apology.

> *You can bury the past or let the past bury you.*
>
> Joe Constance (1955-) Entrepreneur

Resolve. Make things right for your customer.
Thank. Be grateful your customer gave you the opportunity to keep his business.
Learn. When mistakes occur we need to adjust or change something so the same thing doesn't happen to other customers.
Leave them feeling better. Whatever happens, it will be a *positive* experience for the customer if she leaves feeling better than she did before she complained. It is our job to make sure this happens.

EXERCISE 12:1

Keep a written record for one full week of every customer you face who had a complaint and how you resolved it. Were you able to make them happy? Did you do all you could for them? Were you empathetic, did you listen, did you take action quickly? Were you as effective as you would like to be?

EXERCISE 12:2

Find something to complain about this week in your personal life (not your spouse or kids), and actually follow through on it—like a product or service you paid for that did not meet your expectations. Contact the organization and tell them why you are unhappy. Observe how they handle it and what exactly they do. Determine if you are dealing with an Eagle or a duck, or with an Eagle working in a duck pond who CAN'T provide you with great service.

> *Remember, there are no third chances!*
>
> Dr. Leonard Barry, Texas A&M University

EXERCISE 12:3

In a group meeting discuss how to remain calm and how to respond to an upset customer. Come up with specific words or phrases to help make the situation easier to handle. Make sure everyone has a clear understanding of the proper sequence of events you will use to help resolve problems.

EXERCISE 12:4

Set a goal as an organization of how quickly you want to resolve customer complaints. Do you have a "one call" resolution goal? Do you have a 24-hour goal? Track complaints to see how you are doing and where you can improve as an organization.

Remember not only to say the right thing
in the right place,
but far more difficult still,
to leave unsaid the wrong thing at
the tempting moment.

Benjamin Franklin (1706 – 1790) Scientist, writer, politician

If you've heard this story before, don't stop me,
because I'd like to hear it again.

Groucho Marx (1890 – 1977) Comedian

"You seem intelligent, capable, level-headed and mature. That's a shame because I was really hoping you'd fit in here."

Goodwill is the one and only asset that competition cannot undersell or destroy.

Marshall Field (1834 – 1906) Founder of Marshall Fields

13

Teamwork

I was in a national chain office supply store. There were six people in front of me waiting to check out, and the clerk was having a problem with a credit card transaction. About thirty feet away in the front corner of the store were three employees talking and laughing. I call these "employee focus group meetings" because they are so focused on themselves, they ignore customers! They were totally oblivious to the customers waiting (impatiently) in the one open checkout lane.

As you might guess, I'm a fairly proactive customer who does not like lousy service, so I casually yelled across the store, "Would somebody PLEASE open another register?" You'd think I was rude from the looks I got from the staff. One of the employees responded with a snippy, "Yeah!" and slowly sauntered over to open another register. He processed two customers before he got to me, and was not friendly to any of us!

So why do I have to feel like a fool when all I want is good service? Answer: I DON'T, and you don't either!

How many times do you deal with a store or organization when employees are everywhere, but nobody seems to be able to take care of the line of customers building up? This

> *When culture nourishes, service flourishes.*
>
> Ron Kaufman – Motivator, author

is a *major* irritant to customers. My question is: Whose job is it to take care of a customer? *Everybody's* is the correct answer.

One of my early experiences that has stuck with me for the past thirty years is when I worked part-time as a bank teller while attending college. Our vice-president had his private office within view of the customers in the lobby. Mr. Gorsuch almost always had his office door open, and if there were too many customers waiting in line, he would come out and either interact with them, help them if he could, or even open up another window and process them. He was a customer service Eagle, and that regular gesture told us all how important customer service was.

INTERNAL CUSTOMERS

Mike Dale is a customer service Eagle. Mike was a busser and dishwasher for me early in his career and was always there to help or cheer up his coworkers. One night our sewer backed up in the restaurant basement. Mike not only stayed past 3:00 a.m. to clean up, he woke up his mom, who came down to help. I can't tell you how many times Mike's work area overflowed with things to do, yet he would still cheerfully volunteer to help someone else in need.

Many of the best companies in the world have found teamwork and taking care of internal customers a key ingredient in providing outstanding external customer service. They stress we need to treat our internal customers—our team members—just as well as we treat our best customers. But what does that mean?

- How do you respond to them when they need your help?

> *A cry for help is a sign of strength.*
>
> FMC Motto

- How quickly do you get back to them?
- Do you volunteer to help them even before they ask?
- How do you talk about them when they're not around?
- Do you know them as individuals and what is important to them?
- Do you greet them each day in a pleasant way, and are you friendly when talking to them?
- Do you thank them regularly and show you appreciate them?
- Do you compliment them when they deserve it?

When customers enter an organization, they can tell if there is good teamwork or not. Sometimes you can feel the tension between co-workers, and sometimes you cannot help but hear the tension. I stopped patronizing a business where the manager frequently yelled at employees in front of the customers.

In the restaurant business we have a term called "being in the weeds." When a server gets five new tables in his section all at the same time, he is in the weeds. No one can handle five new tables at once and still give excellent service.

Most jobs have times when the employee is in the weeds. There are times when you are just completely overwhelmed and can't do what you need to do to take care of customers the way they expect and deserve. Our work usually goes in cycles; we are in the weeds, then we are slower, we are in the weeds, we are slower, in the weeds… Well, you get the picture. So when I am in the weeds, what am I hoping? That someone is going to help me. Then, when I am slower, my responsibility is to be aware of what is going on with my co-workers. Most likely we're not all in the weeds at the same time.

> *We are most effective as a team when*
> *we compliment each other without*
> *embarrassment and disagree without fear.*
>
> Unknown

Now, THAT'S real teamwork—when we help each other without even being asked!

I've said I believe it's everybody's job to take care of customers. I also believe the front-line employee is the most important when it comes to great service. They generally come in contact with many more customers than any manager ever does.

I was recently hired by a casino to conduct customer service workshops. I went to seven other casinos as a "mystery customer" to check them out without them knowing. As I observed, I found the people who came in contact with the most customers are the security guards at the front door. They talked to almost everyone, and if they didn't talk, it was still the first person the customer saw.

Does it make a difference how you personally treat customers? After all, you may be just one person in hundreds who work for your organization. Does one person really have an effect? Read the following and then answer that question:

Xvxryonx Makxs a Diffxrxncx

Sometimxs I gxt to thinking that what I do doxsn't mattxr. But whxn I start thinking that way, I rxmxmbxr my old typxwritxr. Most of thx kxys workxd finx most of thx timx. But onx day, onx of thx kxys stoppxd working altogxthxr. And that rxally mxssxd xvxrthing up.
So whxn I'm txmptxd to say, I'm only onx pxrson,
*It won't makx much diffxrxncx if I don't do this quitx right, I rxmxmbxr my old typxwritxr and I say to mysxlf: "I am a kxy pxrson and nxxded vxry much."**

*Used with permission from Tom Connellan, Inside the Magic Kingdom (Austin, TX: Bard Press, 1997)

YOU DO make a difference! I ask participants in my workshops, "How many employees does it take to lose a good customer?" They catch on quickly and yell, "one!"—which is absolutely true!

TALK STORY

In the workshops I conduct in Hawaii, I have learned many things about hospitality and customer service from employees who provide excellent service to millions of tourists and visitors to the Islands. They use the term "talk story," which means spending a little time each day talking to your co-workers about their lives outside of work. It is getting to know them as individuals and what they do before and after their job. Taking a few minutes (but not *too many*) can make a huge difference in attitudes and cooperation in the workplace. I'm not talking about getting too personal or loading personal problems onto co-workers, but just taking an interest in the people you probably spend the greatest amount of time with each week.

THE COCONUT WIRELESS

This is another island term that means the unofficial communication that sometimes travels faster than official communication. This is gossip, or the grapevine. The coconut wireless can be a great communication tool for positive things, but it also has a very harmful potential for negative things.

Spreading rumors and gossiping about co-workers is extremely harmful to teamwork. I ask participants how many people it takes to gossip. Many reply "one," until someone yells "two." I ask why two, and they say that someone has to listen! This is entirely accurate. I tell people that if you lis-

> *We handle customer baggage –*
> *they should never handle ours.*
>
> Southwest Airlines

ten to others spread gossip you're just as guilty as they are. Refuse to participate at all. Don't spread things and don't listen to things. You know that co-worker who tells you juicy tidbits about another co-worker? Guess who they're talking about when you aren't around? That's right—YOU!

GOALS

One key characteristic of effective teams is to have clear goals and objectives everyone is working toward together. Does your organization or business have clear goals that all team members buy into achieving? When faced with problems or decisions, do they automatically know the answer because it leads directly to their goals? Do you have a system for monitoring service performance and determining just how effective everyone is? Are you improving or declining? Do you post customer complaints (and compliments)? Do you track progress for everyone to see? Do you reward excellence and have your personal Eagle stories of employees who provided exemplary service and how they did it? Not having clear targets and objectives is one of the biggest downfalls of many organizations.

An important part of setting goals for organizations is having standards of performance for employees. How *am* I supposed to perform or respond to a customer?

I was in Madison, Wisconsin to conduct a workshop on customer service with many employees from a national chain restaurant attending. I went into that restaurant the night before to "check them out" without them knowing who I was or that I was rating them. My service was OUTSTANDING, from the greeting at the front door to the delivery of the check and cashing out. It wasn't just my service that was great, but EVERYONE I observed—from the servers to

> *No one can whistle a symphony.*
> *It takes an orchestra to play it.*
>
> H. E. Luccock

the customers—was having fun. I was absolutely impressed! After I finished, I asked my server how management got everyone so focused on customer service and having a great time. She stopped, looked at me, and said, "What do you mean what does management do?" She continued, "We do this ourselves. If someone new starts working here and they don't do things the way we think they should be done, we pull them aside and tell them that this isn't the way we do things here, and either you change or find a job somewhere else!" Again, I was flabbergasted! The entire team took it upon themselves to make sure everyone acts in unison and "fits" into their standards. How powerful is that?!

DWYSYWD

I read this term somewhere and liked it. It stands for **D**o **W**hat **Y**ou **S**ay **Y**ou **W**ill **D**o. Simple, yet critical to good team performance. When you tell someone you will do something, then do it. Don't make promises you can't or won't keep. As team members we need to depend on each other. Customer service is complex and requires several things all happening the way they're supposed to in a high-quality efficient and timely manner. When one department or individual does not DWYSYWD, it messes up the whole process and the customer (and ultimately the organization) suffers because of it. When we make commitments we need to follow through on them!

As mentioned in an earlier chapter, Confucius said, "The shortest pencil is better than the longest memory." We're all busy and have lots of things to remember in our daily lives, so when you make commitments, write them down. It can be on a pad of paper or on your wrist, but keep your

> *I asked why somebody didn't do something, and then I realized I was somebody.*
>
> Lily Tomlin (1939 -) American actress, comedian

commitments and your team will work together much more effectively. Both our *word* and our *reputation* are at stake every time we make a commitment.

TEAM MEMBERS WHO AREN'T REALLY TEAM MEMBERS

What do you do when someone comes on board who doesn't "fit in?" Or worse yet, when someone has been on the team for many years and either never did fit in, or recent circumstances changed and he doesn't perform like he used to? Sometimes we tell the supervisor, manager, or owner who discounts it, or says it's just a personality issue between you and him, or (by far the most frequent response) just does nothing about it. When people in authority don't care about employee morale, the Eagles eventually all leave and the labor pool is full of ducks. As an employee, what can you do short of leaving?

First, sit down with your boss and explain exactly how you feel. Use specifics, and tell her how the situation impacts customers and fellow employees. Give examples of lost or unhappy customers. Have the manager confirm your observations or comments with other employees, if possible.

Another option is to sit down with the employee and just talk to him about what's going on. You don't have to attack him; you can just say, "You don't seem happy here anymore," and see where the conversation goes.

If this doesn't work, then I recommend that a group of employees approach the one employee. If, as a team, you feel the person doesn't "fit" when it comes to your organization because of poor service or low standards, telling him is a way to clear the air and let him know that you notice and

> *People who get*
> *along with others*
> *get promoted.*
>
> Ann Relph

that you care. It takes a really twisted person to continue negative habits under the pressure of a group of employees who are demanding better service. Poor performers pack up in short order and move on to another pond where ducks are welcome and poor performance is accepted.

The keys with performance issues are specifics and documentation. You need to document exactly what happened and all the details. You also need to describe it in terms of specific behavior and activity, not just, "She had a bad attitude." Instead, put down, "She was throwing dishes in the kitchen and swearing at the dishwasher." Her actions need to be written out to be really useful.

I think it's important for team members to be proactive in dealing with performance issues. Co-workers know a LOT more than any manager as to what *really* goes on when it comes to serving the customer. As a manager and business owner, I depend on my staff to help me diagnose problem employees or employees with problems. I WANT to know when we're not doing well. That one employee will interact with literally thousands of customers this year. If it's not a positive experience for our guests, it will cost a significant amount of money.

One caution here is if an employee *wants* to do a better job, help them in any way you can. It's easy to fire someone when he just doesn't care, but when he does care, I go out of my way to help him succeed. As employees, we need to do the same thing. If he really is trying, then don't expect perfection but demand progress. In fairness, we can expect improvement over a period of time, so be patient with those who are trying, as long as they are headed in the right direction.

> *We are all in this together,*
> *but sometimes by ourselves.*
>
> Lily Tomlin (1939 -   ) Actress, comedian

EAGLE EYE VIEW

- EAGLES are ALWAYS aware of what customers are experiencing at all times. It should be the number-one duty of everyone.
- EAGLES treat their co-workers as well as their best customers. Greet them each day, appreciate them, and thank them. Be a positive force in creating a friendly, fun workplace.
- EAGLES spend some time getting to know their co-workers. What's important to them, and what's going on in their lives? "Talk story."
- EAGLES don't spread gossip or rumors. When someone approaches them with inappropriate news or juicy gossip, they tell them they don't want to hear it, or just walk away. Listening to them, makes you just as guilty as they are.
- Set goals for your organization if you don't already have them. Post results in places where all employees see them. Get the team excited about achieving new levels of performance.
- EAGLES make commitments to co-workers and are responsible about following through. EAGLES need to depend on each other, and one big area that creates problems is when we can't trust each other.
- EAGLES are proactive in solving problem employee behavior. Talk to management or talk directly to your co-worker. Help her be successful either in your organization or in her next job.

> *Alone we can do so little;*
> *together we can do so much.*
>
> Helen Keller (1880 – 1968) Deafblind author, activist

EXERCISE 13:1

Have an employee meeting to discuss "internal customer service." Brainstorm ideas on how you can improve as a team. What are the ways you irritate each other or make more work for each other? What can you do to help each other? What can you do to get to know each other better? What can you do to build a stronger team? After coming up with some ideas, vote on the top few, then look for ways to implement them.

EXERCISE 13:2

Set some specific performance goals about customer service. Make sure they are measurable and can be tracked. Things like how long it takes when a customer walks through the front door until someone greets him, or how many times a customer has to contact you before her problem is resolved. Or what their satisfaction level is on a scale of 1 to 5. Have some goals to work toward achieving, monitor them, work on improvements and then celebrate your successes.

EXERCISE 13:3

Set up an employee meeting with your department or work team. This works best if you end up in groups of five to seven people. If you have forty people in your department or organization, break into smaller groups with the people who work the most frequently or closest to each other in the same groups. Then, standing in a circle, pick one person to start, and have every person in the group give the first person a ten-second compliment. It has to be something you

> *Individual commitment to a group effort – that is what makes a team work, a company work, a society work, a civilization work.*
>
> Vince Lombardi (1913 – 1970) NFL Head Coach

like or appreciate about the person; like her sense of humor, work ethic, knowledge, or anything else that relates to a talent or skill you have observed in her. Limit the complements to ten seconds each, so the meeting doesn't last all day!

After everyone gives the first person a compliment, move clockwise in the circle to the next person, and have everyone give this person a compliment. Continue until everyone in the circle has received a compliment from everyone else. This is a great exercise in appreciating our co-workers and taking time once in a while to tell them.

EXERCISE 13:4

What one idea in this chapter would have the most positive impact on my service and relationships with my internal customers? What is my action plan? What will I do to make the needed change, and when?

Coming together is a beginning, staying together is a process, and working together is a success.

Henry Ford (1883 – 1947) Founder of the Ford Motor Company

We take Eagles and teach them to fly in formation.

Wayne Calloway (1936 – 1998) Former CEO of PepsiCo

None of us is as smart as all of us.

Roy Disney (1930 -   ) Senior Executive – Walt Disney Company

Working together sets you apart.

Unknown

T.E.A.M. – Together Everyone Achieves More.

Unknown

Wearing the same shirts doesn't make a team.

- Buchhotz and Roth - Authors

Michael,
if you can't pass, you can't play.

Coach Dean Smith to Michael Jordan in his freshman year at UNC

"We're willing to do whatever it takes to turn this company around, as long as you don't ask us do anything different."

The way to get started is to quit talking and begin doing.

Walt Disney (1901 – 1966) Visionary, entrepreneur

Summary

So, what does it take to be an EAGLE? If I had to wrap up the entire book in just a few paragraphs, the important points I want you to remember (and more importantly, practice!) are these:

1. *Anyone* can be an EAGLE. All it takes is desire, effort, and the right attitude. It is not easy, and it's very uncommon, but the only thing stopping you is you!
2. If you decide to continuously put forth the effort to be an EAGLE, it will not only make you a very valuable employee to your organization, it will have a tremendous positive impact on your life. From marriage and relationships to promotions and pay rates, being an EAGLE pays big dividends.
3. EAGLES don't use excuses or blame circumstances. EAGLES find ways to make things happen. Even if your hands are tied and your resources limited, you can still be an EAGLE by giving it your all and your best.
4. EAGLES begin by making a great first impression, and understand all the things they need to do to accomplish it. Getting the customer experience started in a positive direction is critical. It also makes it easier to keep going in the right direction.
5. EAGLES always work to communicate effectively with their customers. They make sure to "listen loudly" and ask the right questions to determine the customer's *exact* needs. They listen more than talk,

> *There is no finish line.*
>
> Elijah Goldratt

and are sincerely interested in what the customer tells them. They know the things to avoid saying, as well as the positive things they can say to exceed customer expectations. EAGLES are aware of non-verbal communication as well, including eye contact, smiling, appropriate dress, and body language.

6. EAGLES treat customers like friends and neighbors. They take time to establish rapport and relationships. They understand the long-term value of each customer and how much harder it is to get a new customer than to keep an existing one.
7. EAGLES keep a positive attitude and are enthusiastic about their work at all times (even when they don't feel like it!). They know the attitude they carry with them is contagious to both co-workers and external customers. They also know they're in total control of their own attitude and don't let the "crabs" pull them down. It's fairly simple: if you want others to be nicer to you, you need to be nicer to them. As EAGLES we need to be positive, even when others aren't. We need to be proactive in taking the high road and making things better—not worse.
8. EAGLES find ways to say "yes" to the customer. They don't let policies or standard procedures get in the way of great service. When the policy allows no flexibility, EAGLES tell the customer what they CAN do and give other options. EAGLES also work hard at identifying and eliminating policies and procedures that upset customers or get in the way of providing great service.
9. EAGLES know the best customer service comes from delivering exactly what each specific customer wants. Every customer is unique, and his needs are different

> *The only reason some people get lost in thought is because it is unfamiliar territory.*
>
> Paul Fix (1901 – 1983) Film, TV actor

than the previous customer. EAGLES treat customers the way the customers want to be treated.

10. EAGLES soar when it comes to customer problems and complaints. They are proactive, and even if the customer doesn't complain (which most won't), they look for signs of dissatisfaction and are aware when the service or product is not up to their usual high standards. They jump to action and make it right. EAGLES know when a customer has a problem or a complaint, it's a great opportunity to make a loyal, long-term customer. It's an opportunity to SOAR!
11. EAGLES take care of their team members and internal customers. They appreciate them and tell them so! They look for opportunities to help co-workers when needed, even without being asked. They realize the more people they help, the more likely they are to get help when needed, and the organization and the customer will both be better off for it.
12. Finally, EAGLES always look for ways to improve, both personally and organizationally. They recognize there is no finish line in the race for great customer service and there is always room for improvement.

I challenge you to become an EAGLE in everything you do, to look for ways to exceed expectations. Always deliver more than the minimum, and do it in such a way that leaves a positive lasting impression on each person you touch.

The only limit to how high you soar is how high you *want* to soar, and your life and relationships will be both happier and healthier. Be an EAGLE!

> *People often say that motivation doesn't last. Well, neither does bathing, that's why we recommend it daily.*
>
> Zig Ziglar (1926 -) Author, salesperson, speaker

Bibliography

Anderson, Dave. *How to Deal with Difficult Customers*. Hoboken, NJ.: John Wiley & Sons, Inc., 2007.

Anderson, Kristen. *Delivering Knock Your Socks Off Service.* New York: AMACOM, 1998.

Anderson, Kristen. *Great Customer Service on the Telephone.* New York: AMACOM, 1992.

Becker, Hal. *Lip Service.* Winchester, VA.: Oakhill Press, 2001.

Bell, Chip. *Managing Knock Your Socks off Service.* New York: AMACOM, 1992.

Barlow, Janelle. *A Complaint is a Gift.* San Francisco,CA: Berrett Koehler, 1996.

Basch, Michael. *Customer Culture.* New York: Prentice Hall, 2002.

Blanchard, Ken. *Raving Fans.* New York: William Morrow & Sons, 1993.

Blanchard, Ken. *The One Minute Manager.* New York: William Morrow & Sons, 1986.

Brinkman, Dr. Rick. *Love Thy Customer.* New York: McGraw Hill, 2006.

Brown, Mark Graham. *Keeping Score.* New York: Quary Resources, 1996.

Brown, Stanley. Breakthrough Customer Service. Toronto, Canada: John Wiley & Sons, 1997.

Capodagli, Bill. *The Disney Way Field Book.* New York: McGraw Hill 2001.

Carlzon, Jan. *Moments of Truth.* New York: Harper & Row, 1987.

Collins, Jim. *From Good to Great.* New York: Harper Business, 2001.

Connellan, T. *Delivering Knock Your Socks Off Service.* New York: AMACOM, 1991.

Covey, Stephen. *Seven Habits of Highly Effective People.* New York: Simon & Shuster, 1991.

Crother, Cyndi. *Catch.* San Francisco, CA.: Berrett-Koehler Publishers, 2004

Denton, Keith. *Quality Service.* Houston, TX: Gulf Publishing, 1989.

Desatnick, R. *Managing to Keep the Customer.* San Francisco, CA: Jossey Bass Publishers, 1993.

Disney Institute. *Be Our Guest.* New York: Disney Editions, 2001.

Fishman, Charles. *The Wal-Mart Effect.* New York: Penguin Press, 2006.

Friedman, Harry. *No Thanks, I am Just Looking.* Dubuque, IA.: Kendall Hunt Publishing. 2004.

Fromm, B. *The Real Heroes of Business.* New York: Doubleday Publishers, 1993.

Gitomer, Jeff. *Customer Satisfaction is Worthless.* San Fran., CA: Pfeiffer, 1998.

Harvey, Eric. *180 Ways to Walk the Customer Service Talk.* Dallas Texas: Performance Systems Co., 1999.

Jandt, Fred. *The Customer is Usually Wrong.* Indianapolis, IN: Park Avenue Publications, 1995.

Kamin, Maxine. *Customer Service Training.* ASTD Press, 2004.

Lantz, Roy. *The Care and Keeping of Customers.* Mission, KS.: Skillpath Publications, 1995.

Lundin, Stephen. *Fish.* New York: Hyperion Books, 2000.

Mitchell, Jack. *Hug Your Customers.* New York: Hyperion Books, 2003.

Rosenbluth, Hal. *The Customer Comes Second.* New York: William Morrow & Co., 1992.

Sanders, B. *Fabled Servie..* San Diego: Pfeiffer & Co., 1995.

Say, Rosa. *Managing With Aloha.* HI: Ho'ohana Publishing, 2004.

Schmitt, Bernard. *Customer Experience Management.* Hoboken, NJ.: John Wiley & Sons, 2003.

Sewell, Carl. *Customers for Life.* New York: Doubleday, 1990.

Spector, R. *The Nordstrom Way.* New York: John Wiley & Sons, Inc., 1995.

Spunt, Trevor. *Guide to Customer Surveys.* New York: Hepworth & Company, LTD., 1999.

Sullivan, J. *Service That Sells.* Denver, CO: Pencom Press, 1991.

Timm, Dr. Paul R. *Seven Power Strategies For Building Customer Loyalty.* New York: AMACOM, 2001.

Timm, Dr. Paul R. *50 Powerful Ideas to Keep Your Customers.* Franklin Lakes, NJ.: Career Press, 2002.

Timm, Dr. Paul R. *Customer Service – 3rd ed.*, Upper Saddle River, NJ.: Prentice Hall, 2005.

Zemke, Ron. *Service America.* Homewood, IL: Dow Jones Irwin, 1985.

Zemke, Ron. *The Service Edge.* New York: New American Library, 1989.

Zemke, Ron. *Best Practices in Customer Service.* New York: AMACOM, 1998.

Never, under any circumstances, take a sleeping pill and a laxative on the same night.

Dave Barry (1947 -) Author, humorist, writer

About the Author

Joe Constance is a nationally recognized consultant and trainer. He has owned nine different businesses and employed up to 200 people at one time. He has also worked for an internationally recognized training organization as both an area manager and instructor. Joe has had plenty of success, as well as many failures. He is currently the owner of Constant Training and has clients in 22 states. They include small, medium, and large organizations, and even a few Fortune 500 companies. He specializes in customer service, employee development, and leadership training. Joe facilitates his programs in a fun, relaxed, and interactive way. His client satisfaction rate is 99.7%. He has a master's degree with a focus in adult education from Northern Michigan University. Joe is a lifelong resident of the Upper Peninsula of Michigan and resides in Marquette with his wife Ann and two sons, Adam and Alex.

You can learn more about Joe and his programs at
www.constanttraining.com
or reach him at 800-816-7919.

At my age, I am looking for a one-night sit.

Rodney Dangerfield (1921 – 2004) Actor, comedian

What would men be without women?
Scarce sir, mighty scarce.

Mark Twain (1835 – 1910) Humorist, writer

Want to grow? Hire a shrink.

Fast Company Magazine

What we think, we become.

Buddha

Want More Copies of Customer Service Eagles?

Three Easy Ways to Order

1. **ONLINE** – At www.customerserviceeagles.com or www.constanttraining.com
2. **FAX** – This page to 906.249.5555
3. **MAIL** – Constant Training
   1987 State Highway M 28 East
   Marquette, MI. 49855

Name ____________________

Title ____________________

Organization ____________________

Shipping address ____________________

City____________________State________Zip__________

Phone ____________________Fax____________________

– ORDER –

Customer Service Eagles ____ Copies X $14.95 = $________

Shipping & Handling ______ Copies X $ 1.05 = $__________
($1.05 per book)

Total (U. S. Dollars) $__________

– PAYMENT –

❑ **Charge order to:** ❑ Mastercard ❑ Visa

Credit Card #____________________ Exp. Date__________

❑ **Check enclosed** (Make Payable to Constant Training)

Quantity discounts available for orders of 25 or more books – please call for details

– QUESTIONS –

email: joe@constanttraining.com or call 800-816-7919